Not Now (1975)
Unless (1975)
For the Asking (1976)
Leda & the Swan (1976)
Meed (1976)
Anyhow (1976)
's (1976)
Gratis (1977)
Belongings (1977)
Antics (1977)

Anthology

The Gist of "Origin" (1975)

Editor

Blue Chickory (1976): Lorine Neidecker's
    Posthumous Poems

Prose

At: Bottom (1966)
The Act of Poetry (1976)
William Bronk: An Essay (1976)

Translations

Cool Melon (Basho) (1959)
Cool Gong (1959)
Selected Frogs (Shimpei Kusano) (1963)
Back Roads to Far Towns (Basho) (1968)
Frogs and Others: Poems (Shimpei Kusano) (1969)
Things (Francis Ponge) (1971)
Leaves of Hypnos (René Char) (1973)
Breathings (Philippe Jaccottet) (1974)

VOLUME II

CID CORMAN

AT THEIR WORD

ESSAYS
ON
THE ARTS
OF
LANGUAGE

BLACK SPARROW PRESS / SANTA BARBARA / 1978

AT THEIR WORD: ESSAYS ON THE ARTS OF LANGUAGE, VOL. II.
Copyright © 1978 by Cid Corman.

LIBRARY OF CONGRESS CATALOGING IN PUBLICATION DATA

Corman, Cid.
  Word for Word.
  Includes bibliographical references and index.
  Vol. 2 has title: At their word.
  1. Literature—Collected works.   I. Title.
II. Title: At their word.

PN37.C6   809   76-48282
ISBN 0-87685-276-2 (v. 1)
ISBN 0-87685-277-0 (v. 1) signed
ISBN 0-87685-275-4 (v. 1) paperback

———————————————————

ISBN 0-87685-308-4 (v. 2)
ISBN 0-87685-309-2 (v. 2) signed
ISBN 0-87685-307-6 (v. 2) paperback

TABLE OF CONTENTS

V POETRY

V.   Poetry

Translating

translator's prefatory note:

The versions here offered are representative of different approaches possible. In all cases, however, the poems are pieces that have been savored and put into English originally for no other purpose than to prolong the translator's own pleasure and perhaps to discover some possibility in them for his own tongue. Only where the results seem felicitous poems too have offerings been made to a larger audience. Paraphrase is never the intent and nothing can be trickier than a "literal" approach, for no two words in any two languages—or even within one—can ever be said to be identical. Even such general terms as "tree" or "house" or "rock." The evocations immediately differ. Every language has a locus. E.g., so simple a word in Japanese as "tree" *(ki)* is designated by an ideogram (as in Chinese) that also means "wood" in their architecture: the continuance of the tree is clear. Not painted over, etc., as in the West. As typhoon is not hurricane—though meteorologists confuse the two, scientifically. Words have their own locales. And poetry feels the particularity of each word within heartened and heartening experience.

La servante au grand cœur dont vous étiez jalouse,
Et qui dort son sommeil sous une humble pelouse,
Nous devrions pourtant lui porter quelques fleurs.
Les morts, les pauvres morts, ont de grandes douleurs,
Et quand Octobre souffle, émondeur des vieux arbres,
Son vent mélancolique à l'entour de leurs marbres,
Certes, ils doivent trouver les vivants bien ingrats,
A dormir, comme ils font, chaudement dans leurs draps,

9

Tandis que, dévorés de noires songeries,
Sans compagnon de lit, sans bonnes causeries,
Vieux squelettes gelés travaillés par le ver,
Ils sentent s'égoutter les neiges de l'hiver
Et le siècle couler, sans qu'amis ni famille
Remplacent les lambeaux qui pendent à leur grille.

Lorsque la bûche siffle et chante, si le soir,
Calme, dans le fauteuil je la voyais s'asseoir,
Si, par une nuit bleue et froide de décembre,
Je la trouvais tapie en un coin de ma chambre,
Grave, et venant du fond de son lit éternel
Couver l'enfant grandi de son œil maternel,
Que pourrais-je répondre à cette âme pieuse,
Voyant tomber des pleurs de sa paupière creuse?

CHARLES BAUDELAIRE
from *Les Fleurs du Mal,*
Paris, 1861

after Baudelaire

The bighearted nurse
you envied, buried
sod, merits flowers.
The living thankless
rest between warm sheets
while the poor dead feel
all alone, no one
to bring them fresh trash.

If, at the good fire,
I saw her sitting,
some December night
found her in my room
crushed from the long bed
gazing at this child,
what could words tell her
tears filling those eyes?

(*translator's note:* Here no attempt is made to adhere to the original wording
or form, and yet the basic feelings have been retained while phrasing nearer

to fresh English is brought into play. "After" here is quite honest, for countless versions over many years achieved this result—which is finally a sort of homage to feeling shared.)

ERSTER TEIL: IX

Nur wer die Leier schon hob
auch unter Schatten,
darf das unendliche Lob
ahnend erstatten.

Nur wer mit Toten vom Mohn
ass, von dem ihren,
wird nicht den leisesten Ton
wieder verlieren.

Mag auch die Spieglung im Teich
oft uns verschwimmen:
Wisse das Bild.

Erst in dem Doppelbereich
werden die Stimmen
ewig und mild.

RAINER MARIA RILKE
from *Die Sonette an Orpheus*
February 1922

after Rilke

Who lifts song
to the dead
restores un-
ending praise

Who shares night
with the dead
will not lose
touch again

11

Though the glass
dissolve us
each may see

Once doubled
voices e-
nough kindness.

(*translator's note*: To try to give fresh validity to the sonnet form today in English is difficult—and translation never relieves the poet of an obligation to keep any structural strategy alive; i.e., moved by the very movement *within*. Rilke's economy has been carried over, but with many realized differences—that the language may yield also some of that resonance that charms even as it mystifies in the German poem.)

ERSTER TEIL: XXII

Wir sind die Treibenden.
Aber den Schritt der Zeit,
nehmt ihn als Kleinigkeit
im immer Bleibenden.

Alles das Eilende
wird schon vorüber sein;
denn das Verweilende
erst weiht uns ein.

Knaben, o werft den Mut
nicht in die Schnelligkeit,
nicht in den Flugversuch.

Alles ist ausgeruht:
Dunkel und Helligkeit,
Blume und Buch.

RAINER MARIA RILKE
from *Die Sonette an Orpheus*
February 1922

after Rilke

We're driven
but take time
for what's con-
tinuing

The rush is
over soon
What stays is
abiding

O to learn
not by break-
neck or flight

All comes down:
dark and light
blossom book.

(*translator's note:* Often it is possible to give the illusion of the original by analogous formal means and by careful ear for sense. And always to project some of what it was that moved one to try to translate a poem into poetry in the first place.)

DA UNA TORRE

Ho visto il merlo acquaiolo
spiccarsi dal parafulmine:
al volo orgoglioso, a un gruppetto
di flauto l'ho conosciuto.

Ho visto il festoso e orecchiuto
Piquillo scattar dalla tomba
e a stratti, da un'umida tromba
di scale, raggiungere il tetto.

13

Ho visto nei vetri a colori
filtrare un paese di scheletri
da fiori di bifore—e un labbro
di sangue farsi più muto.

EUGENIO MONTALE
from *La Bufera e Altro,* Neri Pozza
Editore, Venezia, 1956

FROM A TOWER

I've seen a water crake
burst from the lightening-rod:
magnificently, toot
of its flute telling it.

I've seen long-eared merry
Piquillo scoot the tomb
and in snatches, in leaps
of a wet snout, reach roof.

I've seen skeleton land
drain into the stained glass
from biforium blooms—
and blood lip turn more mute.

(*translator's note:* This is an attempt at rendering as literally and effectively as possible the feelings within the music of the original. Montale is a poet of precise language and with an excellent ear—these require tendering. No effort is made to simplify or explain what is rich and evoking experience.)

---

translator's afterword:

Despite all other efforts, the versions offered here are not in contention with any others *or* the originals. Relations are clear and one poem should not negate the other: quite the opposite.

The only test is whether the later work also can stand up as poetry and so commend itself to generations.

There are countless ways and each must prove itself within the specific encounter. No rules exist that promise success or can deny what comes through despite all odds.

Poetry is the measure, as it is the life.

(from *Elizabeth:* XI, March 1968)

Poetry as Translation

So squeezed, wince you I scream? I love you & hate
off with you. Ages! *Useless.* Below my waist
he has me in Hell's vice.
Stalling. He let go. Come back : brace
me somewhere. No. No. Yes! everything down
hardens I press with horrible joy down
my back cracks like a wrist
shame I am voiding oh behind it is too late. . . .

*   *   *   *   *

Strike, churl; hurl, cheerless wind, then; heltering hail
May's beauty massacre and wispèd wild clouds grow
Out on the giant air; telling Summer No,
Bid joy back, have at the harvest, keep Hope pale.

*   *   *   *   *

What demented malice, my silly Ravidus,
eggs your pricked conceit into my iambics?
What god not too benign that you invoked would
care dream your parrot's skit of ire and ruckus?
And it wants to purr in the public vulva?

16

What wish to live it up, be noticed—apt as
air is, squandering in my love's amorous
vice longer than you wished it, marred but poignant.

*   *   *   *   *

In the year's time or less since Celia and Louis Zukofsky's versions of
Catullus have been available between covers, the book has been
formidably attacked in some of the respectable English periodicals
(*Encounter* most notably) and where it has been found acceptable has
been quickly glossed over. The *Encounter* critic is even content to
guess that the versions were knocked off in short order "on the side."
In fact, the brief preface to the collection makes it pertinently clear
that it was undertaken originally no later than 1961. In short, at least
8 or 9 years' labor, of more than love to my ear, have gone into it.

This, in itself, guarantees nothing. Examination proves, however, unbelievable care and a verbal imagination have operated that
will be long available for the quarrying of future avant-gardes
everywhere.

I feel no need to mince words in this matter. My relation as a
frequent publisher of the Zukofskys and of many of these poems as
they first occurred is too well-known. But my response to poetry is to
poetry. A reviewer scans what comes his way and in the short time
given him attempts to judge what is, of necessity, beyond judgement. It would take as much imaginative effort to realize fully what is
here—in these versions of Catullus—as went into the making of this
book. And I have seen NO evidence as yet that anyone is willing to
put in even a fraction of that effort. But judgement is readily passed.
And the readers, the few there are, of open-mind and ready ear, are
prevented from even approaching this "possibility."

Because Zukofsky's work, prose or poetry, is almost
invariably—even by its avid admirers—regarded as painfully difficult
or obscure—I've taken the liberty of quoting one—quite typical—
stanza from a poem much accepted in England (and duly an-
thologized by the Penguin folk) by another American. John Berryman's *Mistress Bradstreet*. Then I've followed by a brief complete poem
by a poet who has also been slow to be accepted and whose work was
regarded by many as hopelessly obscure—once. Hopkins. And
then—last—a complete poem from the Zukofskys' *Catullus* (number
40). I have deliberately chosen a poem well into the collection, for

17

they tend to become more openly inventive as they proceed. (They were mostly done by the numbers chronologically.) All I would suggest is that you read with your ears and senses open to these texts and tell me, or anyone, or just yourself, which is freshest, which is most truly inventive (unpredictable and yet true)?

I find it hard to believe that anyone can be long in doubt who has any experience of what poetry is or can be. The Berryman is pastiche and academic pudding—no doubt the sort of thing that seems to provide support for those who pretend to teach in the upper schools. The Hopkins piece is characteristic enough, but not a piece he himself thought highly of and is amongst his fragments. For its day it is bold and the music varied and lively—but it invents close to being lost simply within the musical play; it doesn't come off.

The Zukofskys, however, in one of the pieces that is by no means exceptional in the whole, a piece typical of Catullus's power of invective in poetry, make a poem that is living at every syllable, a delight to sound. Try it on your tongue.

The critic may pooh-pooh the poet's avowed intention (or even more sarcastically suggest it is meant tongue-in-cheek) in his preface where he says what he has, in effect, done:

> This translation of Catullus follows the sound, rhythm, and syntax of his Latin—tries, as is said, to breathe the "literal" meaning with him.

The critic may—but the poet exceeds the bluff of those who pride themselves on crass stupidity.

> Quænam te mala mens, miselle Ravide,
> agit præcipitem in meos iambos?
> quis deus tibi non bene advocatus
> vercordem parat excitare rixam?
> quid vis? qualubet esse notus optas?
> eris, quandoquidem meos amores
> cum longa voluisti amare pœna.

It is natural, perhaps, and easy to imagine that anyone can do this sort of thing in translating. Try it. I have tried it—tried it actually *in advance* on a poem that I knew had not been done yet (at that time) to see how close I could come—aware of his vocabulary and stylistics—to his version. It turned out that my version bore *no* resemblance to his (it was done, mine, quickly, I admit—and perhaps for that very reason most relevant here) and was hopelessly inferior.

The question at issue is not whether Catullus would have liked these versions or not—though I might like to think so—or whether they have the same weight or speed as the original. These versions *are* originals. Related, yes, beyond any doubt. A semblance of Latin syllabics in English and English itself extended anew—as if the language itself were being renewed in our mouths.

There is no point in comparing these versions with any other versions of Catullus—as if there were an accuracy to be attained in such makings. The only accuracy must occur within the work itself as poetry.

The very fact that it is poetry by one of the few living masters in itself warrants the most scrupulous attention. And the dust-jacket of the book provides the clearest evidence of how much care has gone into even the shortest poems. And there isnt the least doubt that he knows very well the "trot" translations and is fully aware of the best versions and judgements that precede him. The front cover includes—in its marginalia—a key statement that again tells us what was involved:

> I might be said to
> have tried reading his lips
> that is while pronouncing.

I know of no predecessor for *this* effort. And it is worth a moment's consideration, surely. *Why* has Louis Zukofsky "bothered" to sound his original?

Elsewhere he has said—out of Aristotle—

> If number, measure and weighing
> Be taken away from any art,
> That which remains will not be much

and:

> What about measure, I learnt:
> *Look in your own ear and read.*

As so often—he reveals, in passing, the best critique of his own work and makes those who would try—act as editors.

To go back to the question raised. Why has he fussed, as he apparently has, to do what looks perhaps like only a mad tour de force? My answer is so simple that it may seem evasive.

For us.

The answer, the fact, may not be appreciated—or only slowly and by few at any given time—but it will remain *for us*. For those who remain. Who remain to read any texts, any poetry.

However, this may seem no more than blind encomium. The only way I can *prove* the grace of any poem is to quote it and let it register. In this case I'd like to quote several poems to illustrate the range of the work and its astonishing control and imaginative perception—of course, an immensely verbal power. Yet we must keep in mind that language is the most profound of human resources—the most deeply managed and developed. So that any furtherance of it *is* an occasion.

Perhaps most apt is to quote Zukofsky on the subject of translation (from *A Test of Poetry*) and as it happens on the very subject of Catullus (long before, I believe, he decided to do the work himself):

> A valuable poetic tradition does not gather mold; it has a continuous life based on work of permanent interest (quality). This tradition involves a knowledge of more than English poetry and the English language. Not all the great poems were written in English. There are other languages.
>
> There are all kinds of measure (metre) in verse. No measure can be bad if it is a true accompaniment of the literal and suggestive sense of the words.

One of the more interesting approaches to what has "happened" in Zukofsky's mature effort in these late versions is to set an early version (from *Anew*) (perhaps some 20 years earlier) against a late one. This is Catullus VIII (Miser Catulle, desinas ineptire):

> Miserable Catullus, stop being foolish
> And admit it's over,
> The sun shone on you in those days
> When your girl had you
> When you gave it to her
>   like nobody else ever will.
> Everywhere together then, always at it
> And you liked it and she can't say
>   she didn't

20

Yes, those days glowed.
Now she doesn't want it: why
                should you, washed out
Want to. Don't trail her,
Don't eat yourself up alive,
Show some spunk, stand up
                        and take it.
So long, girl. Catullus
                    can take it.
He won't bother you, he won't
                    be bothered:
But you'll be, nights.
What do you want to live for?
Whom will you see?
Who'll say you're pretty?
Who'll give it to you now?
Whose name will you have?
Kiss what guy? bite whose
                    lips?
Come on Catullus, you can
                take it.

This earlier version, as I reread it now, makes me want to compare the
original to a somewhat similar theme-treatment by Horace—but
that's another story. This version—I believe—would not have of-
fended or disturbed critics anywhere and would—more likely—even
as it still does—please many. It is clear and direct and nicely turned,
the breaking lines working well and the colloquial diction building
wit and sense. Yet there is something off—it isnt either Catullus *or*
Zukofsky enough. But they have begun to sight each other through
the haze of a still Poundian poetics.

What happens in the more recent version is a revolution, is
startling. And obviously has pulled up many readers of presumable
goodwill short. And it is characteristic of the work as a whole.
Yet—again—I strongly suggest that you *sound* what is happening, so
that you can both hear and taste it. For me, the latter, later, version is
a magnificent invention drawn from the "literal" sounding of Catullus's text: it is Latin and English singing together and making each
other make more sense than heretofore imagined possible.

Miss her, Catullus? don't be so inept to rail
at what you see perish when perished is the case.
Full, sure once, candid the sunny days glowed, solace,
when you went about it as your girl would have it,
you loved her as no one else shall ever be loved.
Billowed in tumultuous joys and affianced,
why you would but will it and your girl would have it.
Full, sure, very candid the sun's rays glowed solace.
Now she won't love you: you, too, don't be weak, tense, null,
squirming after she runs off to miss her for life.
Said as if you meant it: *obstinate, obdurate.*
Vale! puling girl. I'm Catullus, *obdurate,*
I don't require it and don't beg uninvited:
won't you be doleful when no one, no one! begs you,
scalded, every night. Why do you want to live now?
Now who will be with you? Who'll see that you're lovely?
Whom will you love now and who will say that you're his?
Whom will you kiss? Whose morsel of lips will you bite?
But you, Catullus, your destiny's *obdurate.*

Apart from suddenly bringing Sappho's appeal to Aphrodite
into focus as another relation, LZ has realized all that he had managed
in the earlier version and brought it more richly to bear. He faces the
fact that Catullus is more than colloquial: he is making a poem. One
"reason," I'd say, that LZ takes the trouble to sound his original is
that it does intend to be sounded, is unusual in its soundings. Where
Virgil sounds for orotundity, Catullus plays and nips. Catullus is
quite another kettle of fish. And if these new versions startle, they
dont startle any more than Catullus does to students of Latin when
they first stumble upon him—as often as not—on their own. And if
LZ doesnt get at every nuance of Catullus's sound—an impossible
task—he both indicates decisively what is going on there and provides English unusual vocal nuance—to a degree that I find, so far in
the literature, unparalleled. For rhythmic play, inner stop and turn,
spin on the ball, unexpected bounce within the given strictness, and
within the scope of English possibility, this is all cause for constant
astonishment and, for me, joy.

LZ in his poem "The Translation" (relating to his work most
likely on LXX—which I will shortly quote) tells us in just so many
words how the translation of a single word (*mulier*) becomes in itself a

poem, as he lives the word woman/"wife" back into fulness of sense,
feels as he sounds Catullus himself. The poem bringing the reader/
sounder to bear draws out upon the page particularly and so takes
more space, as it takes place, than may seem altogether appropriate
here. But taste and see:

Wonder
  once
whence
  mulier

woman—
  Latin
mens
  sounds

other
  sense
in
  native

homonym—
  my
love
  air–

mule–
  ier
hardly
  either—

who
  can
who
  can

know
  both
is
  short—

what
    does
    Lewis and
    Short

say—
    (from)
mollior—
    we

homonym
    mulley
or
    also

spelled
    mooley
why
    not

mool*ea*
    l, e, a
why
    l, e, y

spellers—
    of
Celtic
    origin—

U.S.
    a
polled
    animal

dialect
    English
a
    cow—

in
  U.S.
a
  child's

word
  moolea
or
  polled

(adjective)
  hornless
(positive)
  mollis

Greek
  malakós
amalós
  mōlus

(confer)
  blaychrós—
(perhaps
  Latin)

mulier
  (mollior
comparative)
  mollis

movable
  pliant
flexible
  supple

soft
  delicate
gentle
  mild

25

pleasant
   not
bad
   for

authority—
   in
shorts
   so

many
   authorities—
you
   know

what
   authority
is—
   when

short
   each
has
   authority—

Liddell
   and
Scott—
   we

little
   and
scotfree—
   blaychrós

that
   is
weak
   feeble

(adverb)

blaychrōs
slightly
   no

I
   don't
like
   that

my
   blood
can't
   endure

it—
   malakòs
leimown
   a

soft
   grassy
meadow
   amalós

light
   (slight
like
   seductive)—

but
   "a
cura
   della

moglie
   del
poeta,
   che

ha

27

tratto
poesie"
who

has
picked
poetry
from

mens—
moglie
that
would

be
mulier
that
would

be
wife
that
would

be
soft—
a
sleeping

breath
sof-
t-
t.

(Shades of Francis Ponge. Or how each word comes home to
nest—from tongue to tongue fed.) (Shades of *Cymbeline*.)

Nulli se dicit mulier mea nubere malle
quam mihi, non si se Iuppiter ipse petat.
dicit : sed mulier cupido quod dicit amanti
in vento et rapida scribere oportet aqua.

28

Newly say dickered my love air my own would marry
    me all
  whom but me, none see say Jupiter if she petted.
Dickered : said my love air could be o could
    dickered a man too
  in wind o wet rapid a scribble reported in water.

or *mulier* handled again in LXXXVII:

No love by test, my love, 'll air then, time, say the
    care of all my time
  way, ray, wound time I mayed Lesbia all mate to
    my eyes.
No love (faith dies) allow for him whom calm further-
    ing timed to
  continuing more to you as part there repaired to my
    breast.

Because Zukofsky makes language move in its music with such
care as love alone puts out, he makes demands on his readers as such.
This is true. But those who find that poetry is worth their attention
should have no cause to put by the care he invokes. Such poetry
warrants attention equal to the attention that has gone into it. If you
cannot meet it, the lack is a loss that should be registered only for
what it is—not put upon the poet who has gone as far as he can—and
that is far indeed.

One last quote from this collection I would wish anyone who is
concerned about the health and possibility/actuality of poetry to come
to:

The poem is LXXIII (Desine de quoquam quicquam bene velle
mereri):

Day, see no day—choke, qualm, quick qualm—benev-
    olence, merit are
  out—all a whim—fear airing perhaps some few are
    pious.
All men are soon ungrateful, no will focuses benignant;
    the more tied to them more tired (tired) with a best
    of maggots :
with me here who cannot grow wise knowing nor curb
    his bitterness, urged
  qualm mode o quick my one—who that quick knew
    the one me—gone become habit.

Perhaps the best *coda* I can offer to this is what, in the event, when the poem, in manuscript, first reached me came as response. In this day and age it may be considered palpable prejudice. What else is love?

> So "many things" or
> maybe just *one* to
> depress me into
>
> "silence"
>
>> "with me here
> who cannot grow wise
> knowing"
>> hearing you
>
>> sing Gaius to us.
> My *uguisu,* here,
> carves of its own note
>
> and air an echo—
> "gone become habit"
> inhabiting none.

Utano
8 July 1970
(*Grosseteste Review,* Winter 1970)

Corman on Warren on Frost:
Poet Interpreting Poet
>Interpreting Poet*

This essay on an essay is the sort of thing I deplore most, particularly when the poetry, its reason for being, tends to be displaced. But perhaps one such lapse may prove the point of what I have just said as nothing else would—for I'd like to show how a poet and critic of no mean acumen *can* displace a poem by so laboring the ingenious as to lose the obvious and help induce specious readings.

As it happens I heard R. P. Warren deliver this essay as an address at the University of Michigan (Ann Arbor) in the spring of 1947. In re-reading some of Frost's work recently I found this essay tucked in among other papers in the book and glancing through, then examining it more carefully, was appalled at what the man got away with. And since he is one of the most widely read critics in the academy, the need to open the issue has seemed more crying.

The poem (Warren subjects several to his interpretations, but one instance suffices here and all are open to the same point) is a very wellknown one and the more useful for that, "Stopping by Woods on a Snowy Evening." My estimate, inseparable from my sense, of the poem will emerge in passing, but is only tangentially at stake.

Warren opened his lecture, before launching into his longest and most detailed reading, with a hopeless apology for taking a poem apart, etc. He introduces a number of extraneous, quite rhetorical, arguments. It is never a question of whether the critic will hurt a poem treating it so, but whether what he has to say, or feels he has to

---

*Robert Penn Warren, "The Themes of Robert Frost," *Michigan Alumnus Quarterly Review,* LIV:10 (December 6, 1947).

say, serves any useful purpose, brings out more of what is operative in a poem, brings the reader more to it.

I'm inclined to feel that, though most readers are likely to skimp the details in this poem (as generally), few will not feel or get Frost's meaning. The poem is not that obscure or devious. Indeed, I find it remarkably clear and immediate in effect. That is not the least part of its charm.

The poem, to keep it fresh in mind, goes as follows:

> Whose woods these are I think I know.
> His house is in the village though;
> He will not see me stopping here
> To watch his woods fill up with snow.
>
> My little horse must think it queer
> To stop without a farmhouse near
> Between the woods and frozen lake
> The darkest evening of the year.
>
> He gives his harness bells a shake
> To ask if there is some mistake.
> The only other sound's the sweep
> Of easy wind and downy flake.
>
> The woods are lovely, dark and deep.
> But I have promises to keep,
> And miles to go before I sleep,
> And miles to go before I sleep.

Let me quote first Warren's reading of this poem, omitting only his rhetorical asides.

He writes: "It does look simple. A man driving by a dark woods stops to admire the scene, to watch the snow falling into the special darkness. He remembers the name of the man who owns the woods and knows that the man would not begrudge him a look. He is not trespassing. The little horse is restive and shakes the harness bells. The man decides to drive on, because, as he says, he has promises to keep—he has to get home to deliver the groceries for supper—and he has miles to go before he can afford to stop, before he can sleep. At the literal level that is all the poem has to say."

Before going on into his more detailed reading, let's look at this "literal level." Without debating whether Warren has brought out all that is *literally* there, I'd indicate that several points he makes are *not* in the poem and obviously not there. For example, "special darkness" is tricky and there's no need to call it anything but darkness (the darkest darkness of the year, if you will). And whether admiration is involved or not remains to be seen. The poet neither says nor implies that the owner of the woods through which he is passing, or rather by which he is passing, "will not begrudge him a look." Quite the contrary, if anything. "He is not trespassing." Perhaps not, or not as yet, but clearly the idea of doing so *is* inferred, the real-estate "his" scored quietly. Frost says nothing of having "to get home to deliver the groceries for supper." Warren would, no doubt, plead that he is merely humorously giving a possible extension to what is actually said, in order to make the scene more palpable. (And even if Frost himself had told him privately that his reading was accurate, it would not alter the case, the TEXT.) What the critic has done, however, is to stack the cards against any straightforward reading. It is quite clear that part of the power of the poem resides in the word "promises" and this cheapening, for that is what it is, into "bringing the bacon home" image is, can only be, to undermine the poem, such as it is. Likewise, there is nothing in the poem about "before he can afford to stop." The poet (or "I" of the poem, which does have a personal ring to it) has stopped, as the title tells, even if only for a moment. That is the crux of the poem, its pivot. Warren did admit as much in his first sentence, but casts a note of needless ambiguity into the matter finally.

You will note in all this that every point I make in regard to the poem stays entirely within the poem as given. Any reader may, likely will, extend a poem along private arcs ("woods," "house," "village, etc., will be visualized variously by various readers, of necessity—but such differences will not alter the fundamental experience of the poem, or shouldnt). There are poems that relate to others and require the others for full sensing, and certainly a man's total œuvre as poet should be reckoned with, but this poem is a good example of a piece that needs have recourse to no other context than what it itself provides.

Warren continues: "If we read [the poem] at that level, we shall say, and quite rightly, that it is the silliest stuff we ever saw."

Let me make two remarks here: 1) that Warren fails signally to remark the sounding of the poem—more than a secondary matter, despite the strong visual projection, and 2) his so-called "literal level" reading carefully leaves out the poetic (specifically poetic) action involved. What I'm trying to suggest—in both these points—is that *any* poem is, if it is operative as poetry, *literally* profound, vertically dimensioned throughout its scope. Or, yes, silly.

Warren, of course, has offered a straw for knocking over so as to lead up to his deep reading. And so he returns to the initial stanza: "[here] we have a simple contrast between the man in the village, snug at his hearthside, and the man who stops by the woods. The sane, practical man has shut himself up against the weather; certainly he would not stop in the middle of the weather for no reason at all. But, being a practical man, he does not mind if some fool stops by his woods so long as the fool merely looks and does not do any practical damage, does not steal firewood or break down fences. With this stanza we seem to have a contrast between the sensitive and the insensitive man, the man who uses the world and the man who contemplates the world. And the contrast seems to be in favor of the gazer and not the owner—for the purposes of the poem at least. In fact, we may even have the question: Who is the owner, the man who is miles away or the man who can really see the woods?"

The question Warren puts gratuitously has a rather pathetic and ironic tone and I'm tempted to substitute "reader of the poem" for "owner." Warren's tone here also is from above, as though he were addressing himself to numskull students. And the theme he promotes I'd suggest is his own theme.

But let's turn to the poem itself. My reading is so transparent it may well seem absurd to bother to offer it, but I have discovered through the years that the obvious is what most seem not to see, or refuse to believe is all or enough. Frost says, in terms that are rather prosaic, apart from or even in the ta-dum ta-dum rhythm imposed and the rhyme structure (the Italianate interlocking invention/ convention—simple but tight—demands poetic intention): He's at a woods (we dont know as yet how he got there, etc.) and he "thinks" he knows whose real estate they are. Warren misses Frostian nuance and nicety, lost in his own nuance and nicety. The "I think" provides an immediate sound of intimacy and uncertainty—vital to the poem (the tone musingly informal, simple). The poet, however, does know that the presumed owner doesnt live on the land, but in the village, and thus will not catch him—as he explains explicitly in the third line. The poet, in short, has stopped at the edge of the woods on another man's property, is trespassing. Why? For a shortcut? No. The fourth line tells us. "To watch his woods fill up with snow."

In all this I see nothing warranting Warren's extrapolations. There is *no* contrast offered or implied. And I doubt if *any* reader is likely to think the poet (and the reader readily plays the poet "I" here) a fool. What Frost has done is to make us *sense* why he has stopped. And like a wise operator in poetry he doesnt go into unnecessary detail: he lets us join him there, provides space. All that Warren feels obliged to add, if accurate, would be to the absolute detriment of the poem. And patently mean that Frost had failed in the poem—for I doubt if anyone *but* Warren would ever have come up with such an interpretation. In sum: Warren raises issues that are of no relevance to this poem.

Next. Warren pushes: "With the second stanza another contrast emerges . . . Here we have the horse–man contrast. The horse is practical too. He can see no good reason for stopping, not a farmhouse near, no oats available. The horse becomes an extension, as it were, of the man in the village—both at the practical level, the level of the beast which cannot understand why a man would stop, on the darkest evening of the year, to stare into the darker darkness of the snowy woods. In other words (woods?), the act of stopping is the specially human act, the thing that differentiates man from the beast."

Here again Warren in his eagerness to score points and sell his detour to us overlooks details that *are*, as always with Frost, pertinent and injects details that are just not there, nor implied. This stanza and the next, even as Warren himself recognizes, are closely bound and the reader can sense that this stanza has occurred, if you will, as a response to what occurs in the third stanza, where the horse shakes the harness bells. This has prompted the poet to feel that his "little horse" (the intimate diminutive again vital to the tone of the poem—giving a sense of scale) "must think it queer" to stop there. The poet is not making *any* contrast between beast and man, but affirming a relation *between* man and beast. Frost reveals a keen sense of the animal and certainly with no indication of rebuke or irony. Warren exaggerates the points he wants to find in the poem and does so at the expense of the precise details Frost has sensitively selected.

The poet is, in effect, saying that he *agrees* with his little horse; he admits that it *is* queer. He admits the weirdness of stopping there then. The importance of this detail, in this sense, is that Frost avoids the pitfall that a lesser poet would surely have fallen into here: the romantic idyll of a pretty snowfall. (Frost is *not* a romantic, or not ever by intent.) And the poet—his mind not forced simply by formal requirements and thus "filling out lines" (Warren by *not* paying attention to such lines infers a failure on the poet's part)—places the scene with an important exactitude: "Between the woods and frozen lake." The poet is not *in* the woods, but *facing* the woods. This is a distinction, say, from Dante's *Inferno* (which must bear some allusion here). The poem wants precise reading. It is "The darkest evening of the year." I.e., it is December 21st. Shortly before Christmas (and he himself is vaguely given a Santa Claus cast.) We might properly expect "The longest evening of the year," but the switch to "darkest" (suggestive of St. John's Dark Night of the Soul) reflects the poet's strongest feeling, response to the journey involved. The poet here could not be a 25 year old and be convincing. Only a man in his 40's or 50's in the "middle of the way"—would feel this moment so poignantly.

Warren departs from his text consistently, as if he found it too silly otherwise, were bored by it. But if the reader rides with the poem on its own literal level, it yields far more than Warren perceives and yields quite enough. It is snowing. And apparently quite heavily. This would not make the darkness darker—at any rate, not in my experience. The frozen lake (Avernuslike?) does not attract the poet. The woods do. The fact that he is trespassing normally would suggest a shortcut, but that isnt the case here. What we are witnessing and become partner to is a peculiar conjunction of events and forces. Shades of Œdipus at Colonos.

Warren briefly mentions the third stanza: "The same contrast is continued into the third stanza—the contrast between the impatient shake of the harness bells and the soothing whish of easy wind and downy flake."

Again the subtlety involved is missed. "Impatient" is not the right word for the horse's action, or not as Frost describes it. The "Harness bells" have a gentleness—again intimate. The horse connects *both* ways. To instinct and to home (promises). Indeed, the word "promises" *rings* beautifully in the poem, picks up the sound and warmth of "harness bells." The horse is *not* impatient, but gently inquires *"If* there is some mistake." Relation is maintained with "others." The contrast, as this stanza evokes it, is rather between the forces of the more intimate life of society (intimated in the horse's courteous questioning, calling him back "to life") and the literally entrancing snowfall. The word "sweep" (recollection of Blake?)—which is the linking rhyme-word—is most apt and masterful, for it also insidiously suggests Time with his scythe. But here using a more alluring medium of transport.

Our critic cleans the poem up with his, it would seem, most crucial arguments:

"To this point we would have a poem all right, but not much of a poem. It would set up the essential contrast between, shall we say, action and contemplation, but it would not be very satisfying because it would fail to indicate much concerning the implications of the contrast. It would be too complacent a poem, too much at ease in the Zion of contemplation.

"But the fourth and last stanza in the poem as we have it brings a very definite turn, a refusal to accept either term of the contrast developed to this point. . . .

"The first line proclaims the beauty, the attraction of the scene—a line lingering and retarded in its rhythm. But with this statement concerning the attraction—the statement merely gives us what we have already dramatically arrived at by the fact of the stopping—we find the repudiation of the attraction. The beauty, the peace, is a sinister beauty, a sinister peace. It is the beauty and peace of surrender—the repudiation of action and obligation. The darkness of the woods is delicious—but treacherous. The beauty which cuts itself off from action is sterile; the peace which is a peace of escape is a meaningless and, therefore, a suicidal peace. There will be beauty and peace at the end of the journey, in the terms of the fulfilment of the promises, but that will be an earned beauty stemming from action.

"In other words we have a new contrast here. The fact of the capacity to stop by the roadside and contemplate the woods sets man off from the beast, but insofar as such contemplation involves a repudiation of the world of action and obligation it cancels the definition of man which it had seemed to establish. So the poem leaves us with that paradox, and that problem. We can accept neither term of the original contrast, the poem seems to say; we must find a dialectic which will accommodate both terms. We must find a definition of our humanity that will transcend both terms."

All this is very pretty and possibly even stirring and I am not going to debate Warren's philosophy. However, it all seems and is highly personal and remote from the poem under consideration.

The retardation and lingering effect Warren mentions is not so much rhythmic in its governance as due to the heavy rhyme, which is reiterated and met with a closed mouth. The final repeated lines are the real delayers, hangers-on. (Frost, as I recall, was proud of this trouvaille.) The poet in his last stanza makes the beckoning of the woods terribly clear. He *is* drawn and *would* go, but the harness bells, "promises," hold him to his normal course, to habit. There is nothing "sinister" involved—or if there is, the poet has failed to inform us of it.

The "turn" of the poem is most difficult, for it is accomplished through the feeling, elaborated in the slow soft sounds, the thickening snow of sound, that the poet is moving somnolently on. The very repeat of the last lines tells us the poet is exhausted, that he *wants* to "give up," as it were, to go into this *gentle* darkness, quite without rage. But the horse, its kind presence, reminds him that others are dependent upon him, that it is not merely his own life to do with as he wishes, as the impulse, waywardness, takes him. (Something like the end of *Umberto D.*) '

There is no "paradox" here. There *is* a sense of the suicidal, yes; of the desire to die—given, as it were, so lovely a death, beckoning. The returning is not one of violence, or strong contrast; it is wearily, reluctantly, sadly, arrived at, almost passive to the horse's power. The final lines disclose several meanings. The journey "back" is a long one yet and hard. The poet has a long way to go before he will know respite. (Frost, in fact, prophesies acutely well his own fate.) And the echoing lines remind of Keats'

> The stars look very cold about the sky,
> And I have many miles on foot to fare.

The poet makes *no* judgments in the poem; there is no moral or moralizing involved. All of that that Warren discovers is Warren.

Frost has used mostly monosyllabic words in simple lyric end-stopped iambic verses. His triple rhymes with interlocking stanzaic elaboration makes for a Dantescan poem that cannot be fully felt unless sounded. The plodding gait and plain language, as it happens, work here perfectly. There is no redundance in the poem. And the poem lives only as a whole—it is not excerptable. Nothing jars in the poem. The only *hard* sounds are caught in the rhymes "mistake" (drawn from "lake" in stanza two) and eased into "flake." Every word occurs.

I make no attempt, nor should such an attempt be made, to discuss the poem "exhaustively." It is a poem that verges on sleep and dream, on fantasy, on dying. Its gentleness and hauntingness are inextricable and due to the thoughtful authentic feeling projected in exact language that almost lulls us, captures us, in its caressing and intimate rigor. Anyhow, we take the poet at his word.

Utano
21 November 1969

Apron In The Jungle

Marianne Moore
Collected Poems (Macmillan, 1951)

What do you do, frankly, with "eight stranded whales" deposited on your premises? And by the same token, what have any of us ever been able to do with our "white elephants," lacking a state-supported zoo to take them off our hands? I might suggest wallets of elephant skin, or stuffing one to stand in the foyer of the UN building, but somehow these answers, these responses, dont really do the trick. The only satisfactory answers I've consistently found are in Miss Moore's semi-precious, semi-Biblical book. And she has simply (or it seems "simple" as she does it) seen fit to make her menagerie behave intelligently, with unexpected nuances of decorum and such natural rites. They are none of them nuisances; in fact, they are positively incarnations of virtue. Not only the animals, but every living and immortal thing.

Then, there is the other fact, no thing apparently is irrelevant to her (I didn't say "irreverent," though I might have): life and the things of life are of an inextricable at-once one possibility; whether we perceive it or not, she does. Nothing is alien to man (which is ambiguous enough; but let it stand). She gives our perceptions intimations of their powers. She finds manifestos in everything. Seasoned moralities, thanks to her unfailing wit. Like the patina that wash after wash, ripple after ripple, the sea builds into the toughness, not to say trueness, of a shell, creating mother-of-pearl:

> in this "precipitate of dazzling impressions . . . "
> in which action perpetuates action and angle is at
> variance with angle

till submerged by the general action;
obscured by "fathomless suggestions of color,"
by incessantly panting lines of green, white with
        concussion,
in this drama of water against rocks . . .

In this poetry there is no such thing as a vagueness of things, unless it is that: the vagueness of a thing, being called to bear. There is no color without its namesake to particularize it:

lent / to an evident / poetry of frog grays, / duck-egg
greens, and egg-plant blues . . .

Colors are textures:

calla or petunia / white, that trembled at the edge,
and queens in a / king's undershirt of fine-twilled
thread like silk / worm gut . . .

And if she seems drily encyclopedic, I confess I should like to have such an encyclopedia beside me as an oasis among facts.
I am satisfied to own the jerboa of her poetry as my pet:

By fifths and sevenths,
in leaps of two lengths,
        like the uneven notes
        of the Bedouin flute, it stops its gleaning
            on little wheel castors, and makes fern-seed
            foot-prints with kangaroo speed.

Its leaps should be set
to the flageolet;

    pillar body erect
    on a three-cornered smooth-working Chippendale
        claw—propped on hind legs, and tail as third toe,
        between leaps to its burrow.

There are ears, I hope, beside Mr. Eliot's sapient subtler one that can pick some pleasure out of these retarded not-at-all halfhearted rhymes: I'd like to see someone match the music she has gotten out of a hop skip and a jump.
It is said that Flaubert taught de Maupassant the art of close

41

writing by taking him out upon the Paris streets and saying, Describe that concierge going by so that I or anyone would spot her amongst a litter of concierges any day of the week. Well, with this Miss Moore, the faculty has long since been reborn as an instinct, never to describe just *any* thing, but this or that thing. When she has something on her mind, we know it for exactly what it is and she is good enough, in her own scale of values, to report to us what it is worth. As of her neighbor's cat:

> . . . He can
> talk, but insolently says nothing. What of it? When
>   one is frank, one's very
> presence is a compliment. It is clear that he can see
>   the virtue of naturalness, that he is one of those
>   who do not regard
>   the published fact as a surrender . . .

Indeed, if her figures were not so alive, we might credit her with being an extraordinary taxidermist. And perhaps she is in any event: she doesnt stuff her creatures nor her lines, but mounts them nevertheless:

> . . . do away
>   with it and I am myself done away with, for the
>   patina of circumstance can but enrich what was
>
> there to begin
> with. This elephant-skin
>   which I inhabit, fibred over like the shell of
>   the coconut, this piece of black glass through
>   which no light
>
> can filter—cut
> into checkers by rut
>   upon rut of unpreventable experience—
>   it is the manual for the peanut-tongued and the
>
> hairy-toed.

Or to put it succinctly, as she often so alarmingly disarmingly does:

> Who rides on a tiger can never dismount;
> asleep on an elephant, that is repose.

To speak of achievement is too much to speak of things as though they had come to an end, or we could make an end of them. Miss Moore's poetry has a variety of themes, though it rarely harps on any

> with the dismal / fallacy that insistence / is the
> measure of achievement and that all / truth must
> be dark . . .

She wants to shed light, but not at the expense of simplifying mysteries:

> . . . Will depth be depth, thick skin be thick, to one
> who can see no / beautiful element of unreason under
> it?

She knows the mind as "an enchanting thing," "an enchanted thing," will touch it with nothing but its proper instrument, itself, so that what we have is

> like the glaze on a / katydid-wing / subdivided by
> sun / till the nettings are legion.

She is concerned with behavior and behavior's element. For all her formality, she knows that "Truth is no Apollo Belvedere, no formal thing"; yet she is restrained (not *con*strained), sensing that "deepest feeling" lies that way. And yet I find her able to get penetratingly into an open criticism of what she is about and would be about:

> to teach the bard with too elastic a selectiveness
> that one detects creative power by its capacity to
>   conquer one's detachment,
> that while it may have more elasticity than logic,
> it knows where it is going;
> it flies along in a straight line like electricity,
> depopulating areas that boast of their remoteness,
> to prove to the high priests of caste
> that snobbishness is a stupidity,
> the best side out, of age-old toadyism,
> kissing the feet of the man above,
> kicking the face of the man below;
> to teach the patron-saints-to-atheists, the Coliseum
> meet-me-alone-by-moonlight maudlin troubadour
> that kickups for catstrings are not life

nor yet appropriate to death—that we are sick of
        the earth,
sick of the pig-sty, wild geese and wild men;
to convince snake-charming controversialists
that it is one thing to change one's mind,
another to eradicate it . . .

This doesnt strike me as pussyfooting. Or carrying restraint to the point of silence. Or the loss of fire under the regain of dignity. I am struck by a human being and a human bearing.

I quoted the above section at some length too, to begin to demonstrate, if it needs demonstration, that this lady has in her speech, which is robbed of none of speech's probity, a voice and ear for melody. And the language moves with neither a whine nor a whimper. If it doesnt move in just that straight line of one's own expectation, it is no less "right" for the line it does choose to pursue. She puts us on the right scent and does produce a few strong wrinkles "puckering the skin between the ears."

In broadcasting some of this poetry a fairly frequent response that came back at me was, "But is it poetry? It sounds like intelligent conversation, no more." No more! But when conversation is so pitched, and delivered with such nicety, and such verbal trueness, it isnt merely an overtaut purity that is being invoked in criticism, but an ear and a mind that will not be penetrated or cannot grasp the genius of the tongue. For poetry is the manifestation of speech's genius. Let it occur in what shape it will. It will move us also to its shape eventually, if we are to be moved at all.

Although it is Joyce via Dujardin and Valéry Larbaud who gets credited with the "monologue intérieur," it is Miss Moore who should be credited with the "dialogue intérieur." Her dramatic lyricism is created by her always unexpected metaphors, her unpredictable rhymings whether doomed by some imposed quirk of structure or stricture, and her self-dialogue. No one has used this last mode so much or so well. It almost becomes her structural mode, par excellence, and occurs more frequently in her later work. I mean such turns as:

WHEN I BUY PICTURES

or what is closer to the truth,
when I look at that of which I may regard myself
        as the imaginary possessor . . .

44

or

> . . . like Henry James "damned by the public for decorum";
> not decorum, but restraint;
> it is the love of doing hard things
> that rebuffed and wore them out—a public out of
>   sympathy with neatness.
> Neatness of finish! Neatness of finish!

or

> Certain faces, a few, one or two—or one
> face photographed by recollection—
>   to my mind, to my sight.
>   must remain a delight.

It is a mode accepted from genuine conversation, accepted and adopted. It has the merit of conferring a going concern to the lines, it produces a spontaneous atmosphere of wit and open humor, it is human.

Another complaint I've heard, from a whitehaired lady in a shawl and black straw hat at a Unitarian Church reading when I read "Peter," was: Is all that detail really necessary? admitting that she herself was occasionally bewildered by it, if not altogether put off. Miss Moore has cautioned against disturbing the "setting for a symmetry," "unless you are a fairy"—which, I confess, I am not. But I suppose one can pull off the various legs of her images and imagine one will find a certain essential weight at the end that is the core of the poem, as it were. But it is as deceptive as the onion (and as fragrant and flagrant in the undressing) or like picking a card at a time (jackstraw-style) from a cardhouse one has made, to test its endurance (without daring to breathe too much). Well, suddenly we discover we are not dealing with excess at all and at a single detracting stroke, we have on our hands simply a pack of undefined tricks. No, it is she who has the "feather touch," who can ripple the keys as well as the inventor of "Aint Misbehavin." Remove a syllable and you remove an essence, a music, sense. And I am as critical of Miss Moore's "self-inspection," as she is of others'. I admit that a shard may have a charm of its own and, in some cases, may remove certain (strictly-speaking) blemishes—but there are times when blemishes are the bloom of the fruit.

What are all these details worth really? It might be asked too,

45

what is reality worth? Something has been sighted, seen. This lady leads us through her jungle, and we trust her: she may not go straight through; she may pause to put some order into things as she passes, i.e., a human order—but after she has gone, she knows it is the mind alone that retains the given order; she learns her discipline from the discipline of things and would have shocked romantic Wordsworth by her being "unignorant, modest and unemotional, and all emotion." When she picks an object up, she turns it to let her light shape it or so it seems. Actually she is eccentric, crotchety, finicky, almost persnickety—but it takes peculiar vision to illuminate our own. I dont go to poetry as to a mirror; I go there for the reassurance of someone else's reflection and find myself and my world in its refraction. She has said it: "The I of each is to the I of each a kind of fretful speech."

It is difficult ground it may seem, to base oneself on; but then one is supposed to get a move on; not to plant oneself so rigidly in the ground like a self-appointed monument. Yesterday in the Métro there was the boy who tripped in going up the staircase into daylight and looked back to see if the step had moved that launched his fall. But no—it was just where it should have been, though he was not. It was nothing though; he excused himself without a thought. One seems to be fighting against one's own inertia constantly in this world of things and beings. So with this poetry: it is a ground for motion, is explicit, like a staircase, for motion, bringing one up or down, as the case may be. The intricacies are part of a passage and when, if one falls, one rises, one may come to realize that there is a confusion of faults, "life's faulty excellence" perhaps.

I dont know that "a tuned reticence," "nonchalances of the mind," a "fountain by which sparkling gems are split," may not lack certain themes. Certain efforts. But when I read a poetry, I prefer to read what it is and consider *that*, not worry about what *I* would have done (I have my own chances).

Yes, I am not smitten with some of this lady's conclusions, some of her moralities, sometimes they seem not merely arbitrarily come at (how else are they to arrive in the poetic logic of things?), but that they are somewhat too pat, too neat, almost at times too trite, too meager for what precedes them, as the close of "The Labours of Hercules" or "In Distrust of Merits" or even the Housmanlike close of "Nevertheless." But she can be so startingly successful, so right, as in "The Pangolin." Or in "The Mind Is an Enchanting Thing," where a

46

where a series of definitions in her inimitable style, with the virtuosity of some poetic Paganini, invoked by the form, "It is," ends with a negative definition:

It's / not a Herod's oath that cannot change.

She does not write from the verge of an agony; and indeed when she approaches the brim, as in her war poems, she is for me least effective, even least true. She is sentimental, overinsistent. But when she is good, she is very good, and she has kept for us little that is not good. Or what is less good is inseparable from what is excellent.

At bottom there is a Yankee ingenuity in her husbandry of quotation; there is thrift of passion, not drift. But her language, if precise, is not parsimonious, no more than Thoreau's: she understands what she wants to say and is not afraid to say it, "this fossil flower concise without a shiver, / intact when it is cut, / damned for its sacrosanct remoteness." It is the same ingenuity that engineers not only the most unlikely resemblances into the aptest quickenings of relation, but brings to bear the authentic vigor of speech (almost an anthological passion for speech abounds). So that she can say, and does, of ""Poetry": "I, too, dislike it: there are things that are important beyond all this fiddle." But that's no scraping on the viol: when she uses such words, there is sense and music in it. She can speak of a cat (and of us at the same time from her vantage-point) in terms of other creatures with such exactitude of language that suddenly each word becomes an active thing, a live thing, again:

> . . . placing a forked stick on either
> side of its innocuous neck; one need not try to stir
> him up; his prune-shaped head and alligator eyes are
>   not a party to the
>   joke. Lifted and handled, he may be dangled like an
>   eel or set
>
> up on the forearm like a mouse . . .

Restraint? Yes; but not submission, not hypocrisy:

> To tell the hen: fly over the fence, go in the wrong
>   way in your perturba-
>   tion—this is life; to do less would be nothing but
>   dishonesty.

47

If there are great ranges of experience that she seems to leave uninvaded, so be it. She has done what she could do and done it with unrelenting finish: perhaps "justice" would be the truest word. If such terminology isnt subject to the "clashed edges of two words that kill," she might be considered as Quaker baroque. In such a frame she has cleared a lot of ground for us who follow; she has demonstrated the effectiveness of polysyllabic language in poetry, which only the Greeks had brought so effectively into play before her; she has refined the ear of rhyme with almost every conceivable kind of byplay; she has extended, along with others like Pound and Williams, the possibilities of the prose-line in poetry; she has enriched the life of metaphor with unexampled resourcefulness and perception; she brings an elegant restraint into successful wit; she not only knows how to talk, but when to talk. There is no need to rub salt into this wound of praise; it is open enough.

This realist in her black panoramic hat presides over circumstance imaginatively. When one speaks as well as she does, one's imagination is the complement. To pretend to measure her stature, apart from offending her dictum, would be to pretend to be fame's couturier and even Paris doesnt prompt me to that claim. What there is here, is what there is. She has spoken with care, with respect, with imagination, and out of her own heart. I would like to bring LaFontaine out of Père Lachaise, where I paid him my respects just yesterday, to Miss Moore's gemsplitting fountain. He would be refreshed and satisfied. Even illuminated by what she can bestow.

Paris
2nd November 1955
(from *Origin* 1st series No. 18, Winter-Spring 1956)

Commensurate Language

William Carlos Williams
The Desert Music (Random House, 1954)
Journey to Love (Random House, 1955)

I think it was Charles Olson who said, after two elderly New England ladies quietly removed themselves from the atmosphere of one of his poems dealing with sodomy, at a reading some years ago: "What have the old got, if they havent got courage?"

The young are another story. And not easy to grasp or pleasant. But what concerns me here is the life put on the page as poetry, recently, by Dr. Williams. I suppose it best to recognize him at once as a young old man, not so unlike Yeats who discovered the thrust of his body most as his life ran out in gyres. The corkscrew intellect.

This is poetry of a man defending himself against the encroachment of death. And not a poem amongst them but bears the blows, many delivered at close range. Antæus. Jacob. There are the myths. There is the man.

He had begun, to judge his poetry by his poetry (but leaving the verdict open to whoever comes), with eyes attentive to just their limits and that precision known at the edge of the scalpel. Although the stethoscope makes better sense. Say, the eye as stethoscope. To see, against the skin, to hear, the core. Say it, "no idea but in things!" And it recurs less as a litany or lament than as a reiterated discovery. Discovering. Taking the veil off the April landscape, finding beauty in the saying of seeing what there is, the "many . . . things of little value" and the bearers of such things "naked as their mothers bore them." I suppose it is childlike, where only the child is to be credited with seeing freshness in things. "During that time I walked among the trees which was the most beautiful thing which I had ever seen . . . "

49

Like a cylindrical tank fresh silvered
upended on the sidewalk to advertise
some plumber's shop, a profusion
of pink roses bending ragged in the rain—
speaks to me of all gentleness and its
enduring . . .

It was not that he had so much to say, but his eyes were full each day and he had, as he has, the capacity for speech. All that any poetry discovers is life and the shape that art puts on is only and always, when it goes, the inescapably human element. The imagination enjoins us, encourages. Art invents us with its kind machineries.

"As in all machines its [poetry's] movement is intrinsic, undulant, a physical more than a literary character. In a poem this movement is distinguished in each case by the character of the speech from which it arises.

"Therefore each speech having its own character the poetry it engenders will be peculiar to that speech also in its own intrinsic form. The effect is beauty, what in a single object resolves our complex feelings of propriety. One doesn't seek beauty. All that an artist or a Sperry can do is to drive toward his purpose, in the nature of his materials; not to take gold where Babbitt metal is called for; to make: make clear the complexity of his perceptions in the medium given him by inheritance, chance, accidents or whatever it may be to work with according to his talents and the will that drives them . . . "

There is much in Dr. Williams that is contradictory. He has said, "To me all sonnets say the same thing of no importance." Yet as an editor he accepted a wellmade sonnet by Yvor Winters. He has argued "speech" the center of any true poetry, yet has praised very highly a sonnet by Pound, a translation to be sure, using highly archaic diction. But the truth, as much as anything can be bothered about being "true," is that it is language of which one creates, whatever sense of it one has. I find throughout Dr. Williams' work a variety of unlikely phrases, unlikely in anything but the "written" word:

No one was there
save only for
the food . . .

All *that which* makes the pear ripen
or the poet's line
come true! . . .

Yet the "rightness" of his usage is immediately apparent, transparent, not only to the eye, but to the ear, which on the page is an inner instrument. To appropriate with.

But to break through and past the good Doctor's overt concern with a "variable measure" into his accomplishment requires very little but an open ear and such mind as pleasures from exquisite usage of language. His gift is entirely there at our behest. What is there to say when a man speaks so unmitigatedly clear, when the push of his words makes music, moves?

. . . It is ridiculous
what airs we put on
to seem profound
while our hearts
gasp dying
for want of love . . .

Consider the dying poet singing his Prothalamion on his death bed! The passion holds us; the language comes with such pure direction. Rimbaud's "thought catching hold of thought and pulling." It is no longer gathering flowers in May, but a winter bouquet that strikes all the deeper by its seeming unseasonableness. But one doesnt question a flower; one accepts it, if one can.

Reading Shakespeare recently in a classroom of foreign students, whose knowledge of English demanded some kind of translation, I realized more clearly than ever before that what that man did belongs to the untranslatable genius of his tongue. Without equal devotion it is impossible to come away with any fire.

Yes, before I get hammered down, it is rhetoric, if you like. How can language taking shape be anything if not a rhetoric? A syntaxis. But not the rhetoric, but the plunge into the reach of the stuff is what gets me. (Cloth is necessarily made of woven thread, or best so.)

. . . what dreams may come
When we have shuffled off this mortal coil
Must give us pause—there's the respect
That makes calamity of so long life . . .

51

There is a weight of consideration in the syllables and in their juncture. And in Dr. Williams' poetry, take it at whatever end, or beginning, you like, there is a language continually drawn out, the thread out of the body, to catch us, to catch our breaths. Or consider the careful meditativeness of the Hamlet. Go scan the blank verse. Go and catch a falling star!

Measure? Go measure the size of a voice! Or speech. Or tell Karl Shapiro the metrics of *The Cantos* so that he may be convinced that that is poetry and not the deaf and echoing schemes by which he and the Audenists rob time.

It is nice to be certain. To be sure beyond the epitaph. But it is wholly irrevelant, if the work has not made it, if it cannot stand in its own right. It would be foolish and rash to announce that these poems are perfect. But perfection is the shine on the fruit and doesnt ensure our nourishment, or growth. The act of the poem draws our responses, or nothing.

"Only the imagination is real!" he shouts. Only the imagination can create the real, can give us our sense and senses back, back and forward.

It is at the bare edge of life that all these poems have come into being. They are sentiment now, unabashedly. Because of the outbreak, the rationale of some makeshift structure to keep it from simply slackness seemed indicated and was found. The triple-tiered line is remarkably fluent and flexible and is open to the varieties of his moods; in fact, it implies a various inner movement, flux within flux, so that there is no attempt at a usual narrative form, but digressions within the form, but sustained by a returning margin. The mind suggests the mind at every turn. (Whether such structure is a vital necessity to such purpose is questionable. I suspect there are other equally possible ways to incorporate such turnings without a loss of freshness and fluency. But the point is that this way is its own success and needs no further proof.)

Matera
21 April 1956
(from *Origin* 1st series, No. 19, Summer 1956)

Hart Crane

Hart Crane is the very instance of American incoherence. Yet in his declaration, published in 1929, about 3 years before his premature death, he wrote with startling clarity:

> The poet's concern must be, as always, self-discipline toward a formal integration of experience. For poetry is an architectural art, based not on Evolution or the idea of progress, but on the articulation of the contemporary human consciousness *sub specie æternitatis,* and inclusive of all readjustments incident to science and other shifting factors related to that consciousness.

And he notes, with perspicuity, that:

> A great deal of modern painting is as independent of any representational motive as a mathematical equation; while some of the most intense and eloquent current verse derives sheerly from acute psychological analysis, quite independent of any dramatic motivation.

And he might be speaking of Robert Lowell or Robert Creeley, if we lacked the date. But it also suggests the direction Crane himself was pursuing and was likely to have pursued, if he could have found enough to sustain him in the world he was committed to.

The author of *The Bridge* and *White Buildings* certainly felt the "architectural" element as his own. If he was essentially concerned with making a temple out of a bridge and a crypt out of the skyscrapers, *Key West*—his final sheaf, as the event has turned out—opens to less flourish and the exactitudes of voice, climate, flora and fauna, and the reaches of highly localized man.

In Crane there was from the very start two "veins" that seem almost contradictory, almost schizophrenic. There is the quiet tense lyric of painful relation or gentle regard, often projected with remarkable directness, despite the poetic stance assumed:

GARDEN ABSTRACT

The apple on its bough is her desire,—
Shining suspension, mimic of the sun.
The bough has caught her breath up, and her voice,
Dumbly articulate in the slant and rise
Of branch on branch above her, blurs her eyes.
She is prisoner of the tree and its green fingers.

And so she comes to dream herself the tree,
The wind possessing her, weaving her young veins,
Holding her to the sky and its quick blue,
Drowning the fever of her hands in sunlight.
She has no memory, nor fear, nor hope
Beyond the grass and shadows at her feet.

I'm naturally brought to comparing this with the well known early piece by Pound, which certainly was familiar to Crane—though there is nothing that suggests decisive influence, nor is that at issue here.

THE TREE

I stood still and was a tree amid the wood
Knowing the truth of things unseen before,
Of Daphne and the laurel bow
And that god-feasting couple olde
That grew elm-oak amid the wold.
'Twas not until the gods had been
Kindly entreated and been brought within
Unto the hearth of their heart's home
That they might do this wonder-thing.
Nathless I have been a tree amid the wood

54

And many new things understood
That were rank folly to my head before.

The comparison reveals helpfully how intense and personal Crane is even in a poem where there is no first person and where attention is entirely given to description of another. We feel a tender and abortive relation involved, a tenuousness that the entwining imagery draws up. In Pound's poem the "distance" is notable—all the more so in that the poet is young. It is a program, indeed, of the mask, of *Personæ*. The need of imaginative projection. In terms of the way the poems are made, Pound has more grace of movement, for the lines in his poem pull together, even though there are echoes backward to Yeats and forward to Frost—though backward and forward in such work loses meaning. Both poems are written with a care that makes them seem almost like translations out of another tongue. Neither poet seems wholly "in voice." Both are playing poet. Pound's poem translates an idea into feeling, whereas Crane's never quite moves from feeling into idea. Crane's tree implies impossible distance, the unreachable. Pound's tree is the image of the apprehensible in imagination, the meaning of mythology. Both are rhetorical; i.e., too language-heavy. Crane's rhetoric has more inertia. Pound's emulates an Italianate flow. Neither feels forced to adhere to rhyme, but merely to evoke it.

Much more could be said, but the reader is alerted. More typical of what we think *is* Crane would be the piled-up shifting metaphorical language, verbal gorgeousness outrunning sense, of:

> (Let sphinxes from the ripe
> Borage of death have cleared my tongue
> Once and again; vermin and rod
> No longer bind. Some sentient cloud
> Of tears flocks through the tendoned loam:
> Betrayed stones slowly speak.)

Vallejo seems incipient. And Rimbaud's love of shock of language, of mere verbality. And Thomas in his even tighter conjunctions. This impulse towards mobbing sense is of our time.

Anyone who thinks to analyze Crane's metaphorical procedure into meaning will be sadly off the mark. Thomas's words and much more Empson's yield nicely to such an approach and tell thereby the analytical effort the poets put in. But Crane's metaphors are invariably for immediate effect and of an immediately dissolving effect—not unlike effervescence. The incongruities of language, the downright "errors," are of less import than the precipitate quality involved, the willingness to project *mélange adultère de tout*: as if only thus could the rapture of confusion and progress in all its vulgarity be "screened" for us. Of battleships booming or aircraft carriers letting go:

> Regard the moving turrets! From grey decks
> See scouting griffons rise through gaseous crepe
> Hung low . . . until a conch of thunder answers
> Cloud-belfries, banging, while searchlights, like fencers,
> Slit the sky's pancreas of foaming anthracite
> Toward thee, O Corsair of the typhoon,—pilot, hear!
> Thine eyes bicarbonated white by speed, O Skygak, see
> How from thy path above the levin's lance
> Thou sowest doom thou hast nor time nor chance
> To reckon—as thy stilly eyes partake
> What alcohol of space . . .! Remember, Falcon-Ace,
> Thou hast there in thy wrist a Sanskrit charge
> To conjugate infinity's dim marge—
> Anew. . . !

This is of an innocence more raw than Apollinaire would have cared to muster, a deliberately "barbaric yawp" of modernity. Carelessness is almost programmatic of American prodigality. Crane is a verbal spendthrift—all the more to be noted, for he also has the capacity for unusual concentrations and densities, when so driven, as when he writes "At Melville's Tomb":

> Compass, quadrant and sextant contrive
> No farther tides . . . High in the azure steeps
> Monody shall not wake the mariner.
> This fabulous shadow only the sea keeps.

Much of the energetic stance derives from an instinct for verbal dress and decoration of the same order as Rembrandt's lifelong joy of old raiment, of old glitter and glamor. Something to relieve the duller insistences of days and nights. Sense of a more expansive era: dream era. A smile that no one quite believes, nor is yet quite ready or willing to abandon either. Mother-of-pearl inlay. Or star-spangled banner.

There is a feeling in bravura, of command. Pound has some of the same manner, though with more learned grace—at least, in comparison. Crane was always an American tourist in Europe, but Pound was the displaced man of letters.

The vague impulse to sing out, combined with a curious diffidence with women, creates much of the range of the man's work.

How much of Rimbaud's drunken boat spills over into Crane's "Ave Maria" and "The Dance." The quest is always towards lost paradise and America—even despite Crane's passionate desire—only turns more lost in his hands.

And how often "hands" enter his work—again like Rembrandt, but delineated always for a tender mood, caressing, mothering a tenderness.

The questions, always rhetorical, that beset Crane hang open, more open than he wants to see:

> How many dawns, chill from his rippling rest
> The seagull's wings shall dip and pivot him,
> Shedding white wings of tumult, building high
> Over the chained bay waters Liberty . . .

The invocation has elevation to lift us with it in. And the image a clarity that assists the spirit to join it. But the question begs eternity:

> . . . Deity's young name
> Kinetic of white choiring wings . . . ascends.

> Migrations that must needs void memory . . .

> So to thine Everpresence, beyond time . . .

Crane's "method," though it is apparently enough instinctive, is the "dissolve," metaphor into metaphor fusing towards what he hopes—not unlike Melville's epic impulse towards Homeric analogy, but this time with a magician's economy of deceptive and catching gesture—will provide "sweep" scope and depth. Hard not to think of the Hollywood adjectives: "Colossal," "magnificent," "the greatest," etc. And so many of his images are translations of these notions of the wondrous and the terrific into stenographic notations of sensual appeal.

Crane writes at speed. You cannot write poetry like most of *The*

Bridge slowly; it pours out. The movement of the verse reveals the inner impulse of the poet. The slackness of the verse, say, in "Indiana," though apt enough for its occasion, as interlude and illustration of a tenderer movement, is already too soft and feels often verbally compromised. As if the poet wanted the section, or something like it, there—but had no patience to see it through.

So much of America's youthful poetic aspirations are in this work: the desire to make the myth, the lost frontier, the placelessness, the material insistences, the obscure wealth of things, the rich confusions, the wild heritage drawn to a vague hymn of natural instincts and enduring vitality. To draw from Europe the best, but grained by the fresher, even savage, energies of the "New World." It is sentimental, often. Gush. But the power that remains somehow in it is also unmistakable, incorrigible, childish—if you wish—impossible to be anything else but American. And so in the line of Walt. Hart.

Hart. That Harold Hart Crane so abbreviated his name is not and could not be irrelevant to his poetic bearing. His mother's name balancing that of his father's. The heart's hart against the white bird, the gaunt machine, the winged effort transformed into mechanism. He knew his name, lived it. And died it too.

The poem to his mother, "Royal Palm," lacks Valéry's intellectual scope and smoothness; it could never have wished them. But it is part of a growing voice, part of the work that promised most—the image maintained and seen through into: the palm, grazing

horizons, launched above

Mortality—ascending emerald-bright,
A fountain at salute, a crown in view—
Unshackled, casual of its azured height
As though it soared suchwise through heaven too.

This is extension of *The Bridge*'s final notes, the Bridge itself extended. And the soaring image so often recurring—again lost paradise of masculinity—as in "The Broken Tower," which reverberates in Stevens variously:

What I hold healed, original now, and pure . . .

(Shades of Hopkins!)

And builds, within, a tower that is not stone
(Not stone can jacket heaven)—but slip
Of pebbles—visible wings of silence sown
In azure circles, widening as they dip
(Downward to darkness, on extended wings?)

No:

The matrix of the heart, lift down the eye
That shrines the quiet lake and swells a tower . . .
The commodious tall decorum of that sky
Unseals her earth, and lifts love in its shower.

As so often the poet writes his own critique:

My word I poured . . .

And even as later Creeley began from Crane's agony, failure of love's relation, the Hamlet role brought nearer home:

And so it was I entered the broken world
To trace the visionary company of love, its voice . . .

Or back towards the bell-call, bell-Christ: God's Hamlet:

From pit to crucifix, feet chill on steps from hell.

Both Poe behind again:

The bells, I say, the bells break down their tower . . .

and Stevens' more meditative remembering these (Lutheran) bells:

And swing I know not where. Their tongues engrave
Membrane through marrow, my long-scattered score
Of broken intervals . . . And I, their sexton slave!

Crane remembers Crane before—is it ever "before"?

And Death, aloft,—gigantically down
Probing through you—toward me, O evermore!
And when they dragged your retching flesh,
Your trembling hands that night through Baltimore—
That last night on the ballot rounds, did you
Shaking, did you deny the ticket, Poe?

Already Eliot of the *Quartets* prefigured here:

For Gravesend Manor change at Chambers Street.
The platform hurries along to a dead stop.

But Crane was quick to pick up impulses from contemporaries as well as predecessors and largely to transmute them to his own voice. Whether from Emily Dickinson, whom he was early to admire, or from what was "in the air": the 20's twang of a Fitzgerald—the tinsel and tawdry, fringe of beads, spangle of sequins, skyscraper and air-plane. Motor car and Brooklyn's extravagant suspension bridge.

And the Depression, though never openly referred to, looms beyond the span of his ascent.

．　．　．　．　．　．

Crane suggests intoxication. If he didnt drown himself in the sea, he certainly would have tried alcohol to the same effect. The poems already reveal that—from the quoted passage about Poe above—so fully joined—to "The Wine Menagerie" and "To the Cloud Juggler" and more than a handful of touches elsewhere. The cocktail circuit was in the offing, the big drink simmering towards the more pretentious aftermath we now soak in. There was nothing, indeed, to return to.

And yet *Key West* points up another aspect of Crane absent in earlier work, though not quite unpromised: a larger world of sympathy in the face of obvious destructions. That he felt, however, impotent is registered too in the quieter more exacting language of the last poems. Only the hurricane speaks loud. Man seeks his god there. And is brought down merely, tremendously, pathetically—as dazedly as the dying mule he beats towards water.

Waldo Frank speaks of Crane's reading Laforgue, but conspicuously absent in Crane's work is that condescension of irony possible to a more sophisticate soul. That lack was never polished. Crane remained a smalltown Ohio boy, smothered in the machinations of a world that had little or no use for poetry, let alone poets.

If the times seem to have changed, it was only due to the campaigning of Crane's later alter ego, the smalltown Welsh boy, Dylan Thomas, who flourished in the college circles that obviously were wanting for a whiff of fresh air. And America, for all its educational vauntings, uses its colleges either for research factories or pre-adult asylums for the intellectually lost and the emotionally never found.

60

Poetry is still irrelevant and only gains attention as it gains amusement power and simply *gains*, i.e., shows itself as gainful employment. But that's another story.

So, the overlay between Crane and Stevens—and Stevens was much the older of the two—is instructive. Crane "played" the literary party circuit, lacking the assurance of Stevens, who had all the dignity of a degree from Harvard Law School and a promising career in terms of economic security. Stevens, in a sense, could afford a quiet life. Crane was geared to the more tempestuous by situation as well as proclivity. There can be no doubt that Crane was much drained by the brunt of socializing and yet his natural diffidence required it. It helped give him, I'm sure, a partial illusion of assurance and, in that way, provided the margin for error his work needed.

"The Air Plant" tells Crane even as he felt himself at that late date:

> . . . this,—defenseless, thornless, sheds no blood,
> Almost no shadow—but the air's thin talk.

The poem almost begs destruction; it keenly spells out the failure of language in its image, where loss becomes apotheosis.

But the poem itself, in its metaphorical variations almost demands comparison with Stevens, say, in "Someone Puts a Pineapple Together": (in its section of imaginative changes)

1. The hut stands by itself beneath the palms.
2. Out of their bottle the green genii come.
3. A vine has climbed the other side of the wall.

4. The sea is spouting upward out of rocks.
5. The symbol of feasts and of oblivion . . .
6. White sky, pink sun, trees on a distant peak.

and the 6 other variations: "casual exfoliations" of "the tropic of resemblance," "apposites," "molten mixings of related things." Ways of looking at a blackbird, like.

But the qualitative difference in Crane's "mixings" reveals a constant difference between these poets of splendid imaginings:

> This tuft that thrives on saline nothingness,
> Inverted octopus with heavenward arms
> Thrust parching from a palm-bole hard by the cove—
> A bird almost—of almost bird alarms . . .

61

Angelic Dynamo! Ventriloquist of the Blue!
. . .
Its apotheosis, at last—the hurricane!

Crane's need of the exclamatory is as decisive as Stevens' utter freedom
from such want. But Stevens meditates where Crane virtually
rants—or more truly—cries. Satire is beyond Crane, beyond his
need. There is no "distance" in Crane; his poems are, as it were,
helplessly and utterly within the competence of his innocence.

All poets start writing poetry out of the needs of assertiveness, of
vanity, of provoking dear attention—but no poet becomes poet until
those needs are superseded—and even the vanity of others no longer
ceded to—and man seen within condition, conditionally, provision-
ally.

The travelling man of "The River" (redrawn both to a more local
and unyielding insistence, lostness, in Snyder's "Mountains & Rivers"), images from a documentary film: "blind fists of nothing,"
"humpty-dumpty clods": the epithets remain only too accurate.
Beyond the Rimbaud of "The Dance" "Medicine-man, relent,
restore— / Lie to us,—dance us back the tribal morn!" Beyond a
mother's "love shine." Beyond the sagas of the clipper ships, old
glories: "Blithe Yankee vanities" and the trophies of exoticism.
Beyond even the prophetic vision of:

Dream cancels dream in this new realm of fact
From which we wake into the dream of act;
Seeing himself an atom in a shroud—
Man hears himself an engine in a cloud!

Beyond—and even Crane realizes this, his death and dying did—
Walt Whitman's "long patrol." "Towards what?"

New latitudes . . .
. . .fierce schedules, rife of doom apace!

Towards what exclamations? "splintered space!" "heap of high brav-
ery!" "fraternal massacre!" "unloved seed!"
Crane, like Pound, would make pact with Whitman, admit the
bond of America, of the work made free again, made new, trying to
find such form again as makes sense new for others. Yet . . .

Yet, to the empty trapeze of your flesh,
O Magdalene, each comes back to die alone.
Then you, the burlesque of our lust—and faith,
Lug us back lifeward—bone by infant bone.

Or at "Quaker Hill" the kinder canto, Whitman's bird of comfort
returns, almost with the voice of plangent Rilke's elegies:

Yes, whip-poor-will, unhusks the heart of fright,
Breaks us and saves, yes, breaks the heart, yet yields
That patience that is armour

("armour's undermining modesty"?)

and that shields
Love from despair—when love foresees the end—
Leaf after autumnal leaf
break off,
descend—
descend—

More than anything Tate can muster for his Confederate Dead.
And in "The Tunnel" the gab of a William Carlos Williams
prefigured—dated more, perhaps, but no less authentic—though it
fizzles into flickerings of Wasteland Vedic smoke.

.   .   .   .   .   .

There are voyages and there are "Voyages." Crane's were always
destined for a Carib Isle. Not for the big fish of a Hemingway, but the
tropic storm, the big blow, the heavensent destruction, the spell of
the sea herself.
The first three pieces of the series of six are too well known to
need quotation and contain some of his most incantatory successes, as
well as compressed expressions. Surely his epitaph as he leapt was:

Bind us in time, O Seasons clear, and awe.
O minstrel galleons of Carib fire,
Bequeath us to no earthly shore until
Is answered in the vortex of our grave
The seal's wide spindrift gaze toward paradise.

63

and

> . . . where death, if shed,
> Presumes no carnage, but this single change,—
> Upon the steep floor flung from dawn to dawn
> The silken skilled transmemberment of song;
>
> Permit me voyage, love, into your hands . . .

And still he knows no permission will be promised, the unknowable "woman" of his dream, the mother of mothers, will simply have to be risked.

In *Key West*, then, the strain recedes, the scope comes nearer to exact ache, the nakedness of feeling comes clearer, sympathy is more acute and more lonely. Even so thin a piece as "Bacardi Spreads the Eagle's Wings" reveals Crane's "nostalgia" of the ear, the sense of "company," sitting in a bar with "gobs," talking USA. But is it *his* voice or theirs? He feels their words, but cannot share his own. Here and in the uncollected final poems another voice comes through, larger within itself, hurt open, isolated, gnawing upon itself, and yet capable of the most sympathetic insights, identifying with an idiot, with all the maimed and sick and yet capable of the playfulness and delight of "The Mango Tree."

Much of the rich orchestral business, the fallingalloveritself language, the Wagnerian boom or Stravinsky squiggle of color-effects, drops away. He is no longer playing epic poet or Whitman. He is Hart Crane and hard up. He is near the long hiatus, quietus. He writes in a voice that begins to "look on." Montale might have written some of the lines, if it werent for the lack of patrician elements. "Havana Rose" can be compared for "tone" with Montale's two prose pieces in *La Bufera*. And it is hard to imagine that the Italian master was not steeped in Crane's metaphorical basin. And "Island Quarry," with its broken syntax and clear follow-through, is as near to Montale as English poetry can get—and one of Crane's enduring poems: one of ours, in short:

> Square sheets—they saw the marble into
> Flat slabs there at the marble quarry
> At the turning of the road around the roots of the mountain
> Where the straight road would seem to ply below the stone,
>   that fierce
> Profile of marble spiked with yonder

Palms against the sunset's towering sea, and maybe
Against mankind. It is at times—

In dusk it is at times as though this island lifted, floated
In Indian baths. At Cuban dusk the eyes
Walking the straight road toward thunder—
This dry road silvering toward the shadow of the quarry
—It is at times as though the eyes burned hard and glad
And did not take the goat path quivering to the right,
Wide of the mountain—thence to tears and sleep—
But went on into marble that does not weep.

                    .   .   .   .   .   .

The truth is—there is no truth apart from the actual life lived
through and into others and through them again to others, that
responsibility of possibility, knowing it, the care called for, the
"art."

And during the wait over dinner at La Diana, the
Doctor had said—who was the American also—"You
cannot heed the negative, so might go on to unde-
served doom . . . must therefore loose yourself
within a pattern's mastery that you can conceive, that
you can yield to—by which also you win and gain
mastery and happiness which is your own from birth.

Listen to the cry within all these final poems:

And it is always the day, the day of unkind farewell.

What is death without a ditch?

I am unravelled, umbilical anew,
As ring the church bells here in Mexico—
(They ring too obdurately here to heed my call)
And what hours they forget to chime I'll know . . .

Friendship agony! . . . My only final friends—
the wren and thrush . . .

Where brother passes brother without sight . . .

65

And now "The Broken Tower" resolves, returns to:

> The sea raised up a campanile . . . The wind I heard
> Of brine partaking, whirling spout in shower
> Of column kiss—that breakers spouted, sheared
> Back into bosom—me—her, into natal power . . .

And we know, we know to our unchanging loss, that no one was there to care. O you ship of fools, to let the poet go!

Apart from moments of poetry, apart from a few late poems of new voice, drawn voice, bone voice, sweet kind hurt voice, we know only the word that poured from this man's needy heart. Authentic, if you wish, always, but so inadequate, so painfully unfit for terrestrial voyage. The "inmost sob, half-heard," that Rilke also heard. And the crystal Word.

Of the 20's he remains the prodigal, the misplaced midlander thrown into a hurricane of cheap magnificence, yearning for a chaotic order at first and finally just some simple order for his ardor, something—someone?—to whom he could give himself. Only the sea waited. His failure to endure into more poetry and a stronger, more mature, poetry is a failure of America, a failure to draw him to what should have been "home." And no abstract America, but even the poets of his generation, his "friends"—not one to claim him enough to keep him. His dream we know, for we still live its absence:

> I dreamed that all men dropped their names, and sang
> As only they can praise, who build their days
> With fin and hoof, with wing and sweetened fang
> Struck free and holy in one Name always.

Hart
Crane

27 Sept 1966

For the Lovers

It happens that one does occasionally and as a lifetime's occupation love or come to love, as the act of human being, the sound of words. Dylan Thomas came, and came early, to his trade and his life and his passion.

And in the years just preceding his sudden death he had become the very image of the poet as voice. It is hardly a matter of judgment, whether that voice was too orotund or not, for out of his effort came a renewed and greater interest in hearing words in poems spoken that many of us still enjoy, at least in America. It was only unfortunate that concomitantly his scandalous presence became too soon a legend that brimmed and drowned him in its overflow, though he never forgot, I believe, to dream of a better poem.

It is no use, on the other hand, to say he accomplished a major body of work or did much to break ground for those of us who follow. And yet there are poems. And any poem that stays in our heads, seeps into our hearts, and calls to us to be uttered, if it does not harrow the soil for us, nevertheless bears us flowers. There are, as I say, poems.

Not the poems of riddled meanings compiled in stubborn binding rhythms from "I see the boys of summer in their ruin / Lay the gold tithings barren" to "Foster the light nor veil the manshaped moon, / Nor weather winds that blow not down the bone" will remain to haunt our time and others, but those gradually more simple more gathered poems that later fall to our ears and under them to our hearts.

Yet it is not fair to obscure the muscling weight of often monosyllabic sound, the desire for urgent music, in everything he did. He wanted plethora. He wanted to blow the world down, to strut its stage, to command as well as commend seas. He gathered the blunt rhythms of the past and beat them into a shape more nearly like his roily own, but not for any arcane reason. More nearly like the folk. And he wanted the beauty within him again. He wanted to carry himself, as a bouquet, to many tables or to an altarplace. There are times one must not forget to pay homage to a man's failures, for out of them his little successes spring, ". . . and the heart gives up its dead."

He was vulgar enough to see himself as Christ and hero and everyman, and then in more vulgar humility yet, as "this box of nerves . . . hunger's emperor; / He pulls the chain, the cistern moves."

He did not see man as his measure, but asked that "Man be my metaphor." For him "metaphor" was the way to language human experience into poetry. He struggled and confided his struggle to words. Confined? He struggled to express innocence in the face of mystery, whether that of death or of love, of birth or of war, and found whatever answers in simple faith and wide compassion.

I recall his anger at the mistreatment of negroes in the south and his anger at those whom he liberally abused as culture-vultures. And there was nothing about him of the proud academic. Or intellectual light. He could be comically acute at catching his own weaknesses out in mid-career, loved a ballad whether saucy or sad and evidently relished trying to compose his own. He could, he did, on a platform, break a serious audience up, drunk as he was, by reaching down in back of the rostrum at which he stood, searching for a jug of water there and frankly recollect it was like reaching under the bed at night when he was young. He could read, and did, other men's poems with passionate delight (tracing the rhythms with his right hand) and how many of us were lucky enough to be introduced to them that way! And he was honest enough to recognize that many of theirs were better than his own. But one never felt, or I never did, in him, a competition. Only love. And a necessary vanity, if it needs be said. The confidence that doubt afflicts.

But his poems, for me, are the heritage, those later ones that opened out and brought us, bring us, ring us, back with them to what he cherished of his world of Wales, like the birds he couldnt, as he explained to a professorpoet in Salt Lake City, help writing into them, since they were there, there at the window overlooking the

68

estuary of the Towy where his workroom was.

There he was—March 1st 1950 at Harvard in the New Lecture Hall at the start of his American tours—as I wrote then: " . . . a little awkward, bulky, heavyset, in a black singlebreasted suit, white shirt, black bowtie (much like a musician) . . . His face . . . the most impressive part of his body was quite red . . . his lips full face round, almost gross. His hair, deep brown, was flung back over his head and very thick behind . . . His eyes, which slant sadly at the edges (as though he were crying almost), are piercing and large.

"He tries to strike every syllable and frequently reads as though syllables were words.

"He reads with great deliberateness and with an actor's delivery . . . he has understood and practised his part. His feeling for poetry is sincere.

" . . . little of a Welsh accent left . . . He ended with 'Ceremony After a Fire Raid' and here he put heavy stresses all along the first part. The second section he read straight and in a lowered voice. The last section he boomed, until with 'Glory Glory Glory' he threw back his head and let go with the final words: 'AND THE SUNDERING ULTIMATE KINGDOM OF GENESIS' THUNDER' as though he were merely an organ and were trying to fill the entire hall with his voice's emotion and idea."

He was taken by ripe phrases. One can feel it. And he worshipped the moulded, melded, mellifluous possibility. He wanted his words like a bell to break backwards. He wanted to scatter sound, as it sounded, over a country-side like milkweed or rain. He wanted to tell fortune by the buttercupful. He wanted to roll forever in the grass of first love. Love always first thirst for him. He wanted to be the child that he will for us, or for me anyhow, always be. To keep his parents closer? And yet he was not quite the innocent, quite the fool, and he knew it, suffered for it, and cared, and could say, knew to say:

> For all there is to give I offer:
> Crumbs, barn, and halter.

Knew to say:

> . . . as the heartless ghost
> Alone's unhurt, so the blind man sees best.

And knew, to his own sorrow,

No answer to the children's cry
Of echo's answer and the man of frost.

But he never did quite mature, and this too he knew:

I have heard many years of telling,
And many years should see some change.

The ball I threw while playing in the park
Has not yet reached the ground.

Against death he would rage, and cry no dominion. What are poems but protests against the end, the particular singular shattering end of each. And then, what he never did know, the accession and broadening quiet of a spirit at one, or none. He felt his death coming, had himself photographed prophetically a year in advance at his very grave, but more grievously learned to accommodate that of others and out of theirs his best began. A war brought it sharper home "but wishes breed not, neither / Can we fend off rock arrival."

When Ann Jones dies and is buried, contrary to her nature his own rebels, he admits, and he cannot but memorialize the loss:

. . . call all
The seas to service that her wood-tongued virtue
Babble like a bellbuoy over the hymning heads,
Bow down the walls of the ferned and foxy woods
That her love sing and swing through a brown chapel,
Bless her bent spirit with four, crossing birds . . .

He knows what he loves. He will speak till his language arise to sing praise of the absent one, till

The stuffed lung of the fox twitch and cry Love
And the strutting fern lay seeds on the black sill.

The honesty of his difficulty bursts through, as he finds more and more less and less and nothing is all and all, words.

On no work of words now for three lean months in the bloody
Belly of the rich year and the big purse of my body
I bitterly take to task my poverty and craft:
To take to give is all . . .
Jonah and embryo.

His birthdays draw him to his knees and to his eyes, young already and ready to be young, glistening memories of childhood and further youth. I need not quote such known celebrations as "Poem in October" or "Fern Hill." They are as long as poetry is. Sentimental, to be sure, and full of Thomas's wonderful faith in Anglo-Saxon adjectives. But, and of course, they come alive to the tongue, the eye that sings, as he made them come with his tongue's wit. And any man who would dispute me on this ground must dispute his own heart and breath.

He has, Dylan Thomas, poems for his children, one king to another, one subject to another, where everything is realm and richness, a congress of kings and everyman's children, who "die in unjudging love." His villanelle for his father has only the power of lived event, sung into occasion. He could not intellectualize his despair and deep concern:

> And you, my father, there on the sad height,
> Curse, bless, me now with your fierce tears, I pray.

He concluded, as Shakespeare would have known, with a prologue, only to spell out one by one, rhyming forth and back to his beginning, his ark, his sensed and sensual, his window on beloved Wales:

> And the flood flowers now.

11th April 1963
(from *Poesia E Critica*, No. 5, Milano: December 1963)

For Love of

Robert Creeley,
For Love: Poems 1950-1960 (Scribners, 1962)

Past that, past the image:
a voice! . . .

To start's not always at the beginning, but a beginning nevertheless. Nothing absolute, yet nothing not absolutely what it is, if a word can be kept to its shape, caressing, as it were, its contours, taming it, keeping it just so. No, not so, not ever quite when words find themselves out. Yet to start, as he does, Creeley, with Hart Crane, the very image of the gorgeous adrift, the lost confectioner's son

> . . . stuttering, by the edge
> of the street, one foot still
> on the sidewalk, and the other
> in the gutter . . .

From the start, then, hope was pinned to the word. Pico.

> The letters have proved insufficient.
> The mind cannot hang to them as it could
> to the words . . .

The poems in *For Love* are selected and placed in, so far as I can tell, fairly chronological order, if chronos is ever logical. There are omissions, some of which I miss, but there is a life in Creeley no blurb professes, that was (and is) intricate with his work and part of my sense of that work, unconsciously at least (assuming that the conscious is all-conscious, etc.), must draw upon that, a personal relation. But let that fall as it may.

Creeley's effort, if followed with the care he continually advocates and deserves, is remarkably open. He bespeaks relations to

others, without any attempt to conceal them—with Williams and
Crane and Pound, Olson, Zukofsky, or Campion.

> It's all in
> the sound. A song.
> Seldom a song. It should
>
> be a song—made of
> particulars . . .
> . . . something
> immediate, open . . .

The Williams "Poem" frankly takes its closing "centrifugal,
centripetal" from Whitman and in turn brings us to Creeley's
"Song":

> I had wanted a quiet testament
> and I had wanted, among other things,
> a song . . .
>
> (A grace
> Simply. Very very quiet . . .
>
> . . . A song.
> Which one sings, if he sings it,
> with care.

Which, in turn, comes more recently to Denise Levertov's
"Music":

> . . . a
> singing
> sung if it is sung
> quietly . . .

It would be sad error, if any reader should imagine me interested
merely in noting influences as against what does concern me: the
continuity with divergences along a given still vital line. No poet
who is "with it" can afford to have missed a line of promise. And
Creeley has sprung, no more full-blown than the mythical Rimbaud,
from a past and leads clearly to a future, meaning he is precisely here
with us now.

And, indeed, to touch the present in such a way, as he so often
does, that it keeps vibrating, keeps presence, despite "What one

73

knows . . . not simple." Or perhaps that questioning presented that keeps throwing the listener back upon himself, rocking him back on his heels, jolts. As in "The Crow." But I run ahead. For I want to trace a development within the man's work (1950-1960), as it now stands, moves, addresses me, within covers, within its own order, letting contingencies occur, relations, as they must, they do.

Creeley's poems have as an element, or aspect, to be more accurate, in their development a push toward tighter formal means, a stricter discipline, without leaning over backwards but rather, out of whatever past, pulling weight forward, toward more intimate structure. Merely to riffle the pages of this book "in order" is to "see" it. Signs of it come at once, but it strikes one *in* its formality most quietly and forcefully first in a poem like "The Innocence." To point up, however, what he has accomplished, it may serve to set before it a passage from a writer with whom he has a certain affinity but who tends to work different formal means, Samuel Beckett. This is from near the beginning of *Molloy* (which Creeley reviewed at about the time his poem was written):

> . . . They turned towards the sea which, far in the east, beyond the fields, loomed high in the waning sky, and exchanged a few words. Then each went on his way. Each went went on his way, A back towards the town, C on by ways he seemed hardly to know, or not at all, for he went with uncertain step and often stopped to look about him, like someone trying to fix landmarks in his mind, for one day perhaps he may have to retrace his steps, you never know. The treacherous hills where fearfully he ventured were no doubt only known to him from afar, seen perhaps from his bedroom window or from the summit of a monument which, one black day, having nothing in particular to do and turning to height for solace, he had paid his few coppers to climb, slower and slower, up the winding stones. From there he must have seen it all, the plain, the sea, and then these selfsame hills that some call mountains, indigo in places in the evening light, their serried ranges crowding to the skyline, cloven with hidden valleys that the eye divines from sudden shifts of color and then from other

74

signs for which there are no words, nor even thoughts. But all are not divined, even from that height, and often where only one escarpment is discerned, and one crest, in reality there were two, two escarpments, two crests, riven by a valley. But now he knows them better, and if ever again he sees them from afar it will be I think with other eyes, and not only that but the within, all that inner space one never sees, the brain and heart and other caverns where thought and feeling dance their sabbath, all that quite differently disposed. He looks old and it is a sorry sight to see him solitary after so many years, so many days and nights unthinkingly given to that rumor rising at birth and even earlier, what shall I do? What shall I do? now low, a murmur, now precise as the headwaiter's And to follow? and often rising to a scream. And in the end, or almost, to be abroad alone, by unknown ways, in the gathering night, with a stick. It was a stout stick, he used it to thrust himself onward, or as a defence, when the time came, against dogs and marauders. Yes, night was gathering, but the man was innocent, greatly innocent, he had nothing to fear, though he went in fear, he had nothing to fear, there was nothing they could do to him, or very little. But he can't have known it. I wouldn't know it myself, if I thought about it. Yes, he saw himself threatened, his body threatened, his reason threatened, and perhaps he was, perhaps they were, in spite of his innocence. What business has innocence here? . . .

THE INNOCENCE

Looking to the sea, it is a line
of unbroken mountains.

It is the sky.
It is the ground. There
we live, on it.

75

> It is a mist
> now tangent to another
> quiet. Here the leaves
> come, there
> is the rock in evidence
>
> What I come to do
> is partial, partially kept.

Here we have the horizon as distance, as what there is to be seen, objective, what one sees, more firmly, via distance, to be grasped, realized, a fix: a past a future present, but how things grow vaguer growing closer, impinge, enter, and one leans outward to/at something, anything, solid, to hold and make hold. To add one's own make and take, a little, to what is there. The placement, the weave, of "there" and "here" is felt, pointed and carried. And the increasing uncertainty, as against the fixed "line" first (immediately) established, finds a quiet pathos at the close. A poem trying to locate ground: "The rites are care . . . trace of / line made by someone."

But Creeley, Olson's "figure of outward" (Olson's prowhead, figuring it out?), is the seeker of inwardness, grace, the searching "single intelligence" he early accepted as his limit and to which all his prefaces earnestly attest. One of his most telling "early" pieces (a piece I saw undergo many mutations) is "The Crow":

> The crow in the cage in the dining-room
> hates me, because I will not feed him.
>
> And I have left nothing behind in leaving
> because I killed him.
>
> And because I hit him over the head with a stick
> there is nothing I laugh at.
>
> Sickness is the hatred of a repentance
> knowing there is nothing he wants.

The poem, which has all of Creeley's potent concentrated presence, builds in a sequence of rationalizations to insinuate and then bluntly (but intricately) state an overwhelming guilt, self-hatred. The poem, as elsewhere for this poet, becomes an act concurrent with itself of self-immolation, a release *"in* tension." Some of the rhythmic inventions reminds me of Paul Blackburn's work on *Proensa* contemporary with it. But Creeley consistently brings other men's accents into his own. And often perfects them, gives them a truer pitch. As here. As in the muffled rhyme of "wants" (presaged in the "at" that picks up the "hit") that sticks at the end in one's craw.

A young friend, shown the poem, said, But why does he say "there is nothing I laugh at"? After all, who *expects* him to laugh at anything at that point? Ah, but that's just it: after such an event one wants to, will, laugh it off somehow, to "get out of it." But there is no exit. The poet keeps having to come back to the nothing he has left behind him.

This is evidently not Stevens' "Snow Man," no "supreme fiction," and yet it is one of the mortal twists of the mind, of something that eats in us, that takes a stick to us, threatens us as our own device. Creeley reaches us where body and mind break most painfully, whereas Stevens makes a code of the imagination's reality, a way out of a way in, a "necessary angel." Angel Creeley is not.

There is, to be sure, something of the clipt Puritan accent, a faintly religious undertone, say, in "The Immoral Proposition," in

> . . . The unsure
>
> egoist is not
> good for himself.

that Marianne Moore quite naturally apprehended as possible to her own poetic inventories. So that there is a curious, almost perverse, neatness of finish at times that makes doubt teeter more. But the curiousness itself stops us, I feel, and makes us "go back" to see how we got there, how the poet ever got us into this mess, whether

> . . . My method is not a
>
> tenderness, but hope
> defined.

or

> . . . There is no more giving in
> when there is no more sin.

"The Crow" finds further declension elsewhere, as in "The Operation," where the poet describes his relationship to his very sick wife in terms that make of it a sickness too and justly says at the end

> Cruel, cruel to describe
> what there is no reason to describe.

And one is tempted to ask, Why, then, *do* you describe it? Unless it be to *be* cruel, to flay yourself in public, hurting oneself because of hurting another, the reason in unreason.

The turn is to couplets, tercets, quatrains, small tight stanzas, spilling over carefully, truly, drawn around the drum of inner talk. But no amount of formality calls us away from the inner event. On the contrary, the formal more and more evokes it. The struggle there. For self-possession. And hopefully, also, surrender, abandonment. The pity is that the terms remain those of "contention," though Creeley himself has written me often enough of his opposition to "oppositions" (dualities). The stage is Creeley, the words entering, his, villain and hero and sometimes tired man, Robert Creeley and Virgil's Æneas, "proposing the old labors."

Yeats's famous statement comes to mind here, to get into what, in particular, the poet's work is:

> We make out of the quarrel with others, rhetoric, but
> of the quarrel with ourselves, poetry . . . we sing
> amid our uncertainty; and, smitten even in the pre-
> sence of the most high beauty by the knowledge of
> our solitude, our rhythm shudders . . .

This is a statement that has resonances at least as far back in poetry as Sappho, but in its more modern convolutions it reaches us through Baudelaire and the breakdown of religion into "faith," "myth," "symbol," "belief," on into self-torment, self-questioning, self-doubt and the relief, shortlived and desperate of every kind of drug, hallucination, kick, until the one question "What is real?" (meaning nothing is) comes to dominate modern "thought," as we face the manifestations of science-fiction and the now always less fictional possibility of nuclear wipe-out. Death becomes the hopeful death of mankind more contagiously, as Lawrence had already felt. And Cummings' "manunkind."

But I'm carrying the thing too far. The line that Creeley develops—thematically—relates to Baudelaire, Rimbaud,

78

Mallarmé, and has analogies in Roethke and Lowell and the other "sick" poets of our time. But not one of these has so left the "world" outside as Creeley has. Roethke has always his father's hothouse—when he isnt waltzed around again by the old man—and marshy childhood to fall lumbering back into, Lowell always his father to beat, his family's incestuous inbreeding and "history." Both are case-historical poets: their poems are essentially psychoanalytical.

There are touches of this in Creeley too when he begins to pick his mother apart. But his numerous dream poems are not finicky clinical, but imaginative self-appraisals: the arc remains one of exploration, the inner trying to find "out." The only contemporary I can think of at this moment whose labors parallel Creeley's closely is Cesare Pavese, whose journals (beyond literary and leftwing concerns) are painfully lacking in "things." It is strictly a world of no one else.

So it is notable that Creeley, who has lived in many places: Mallorca, Provence, New Hampshire, Guatemala, New Mexico, has never—despite rather spectacular landscapes—evoked geography or place. His poems are invariably located precisely and only within himself. I can think of no one, in fact, who has more stubbornly carried on so involuted a duel or, if you will, a dialogue. He is, in a sense, the logical offspring of a poet like Baudelaire and, so, predictable. But it takes a certain courage, nerve, and innocence, perhaps obsessiveness, to have maintained so difficult a way, loving the impasse, and to have done so with such high result.

Dr. Williams has written:

> When a man makes a poem, makes it, mind you, he takes words as he finds them interrelated about him and composes them—without distortion which would mar their exact significances—into an intense expression of his perceptions and ardors that they may constitute a revelation in the speech that he uses. It isn't what he says that counts as a work of art, it's what he makes, with such intensity of perception that it lives with an intrinsic movement of its own to verify its authenticity . . .

As in his own "To Elsie" with its sharply phrased thrust-at-us conclusion:

No one
to witness
and adjust, no one to drive the car.

Creeley's original desire to write in Basic English, and he very nearly does even now, would hardly find exception in Williams' quoted lines, but the good doctor exploits an openness of concern, perhaps inevitable *as* a doctor, a certain outgoingness, that one can never honestly hope for Creeley, but only a slow coming to relation, instead, with himself and maybe a few others and with us, in his life, in his poems.

But to get back and on to how language can and does *work* and again how more often it just dont, here is Louis MacNeice's recent "The Wiper" to set beside/before "I Know a Man":

THE WIPER

Through purblind night the wiper
Reaps a swathe of water
On the screen: we shudder on
And hardly hold the road,
All we can see a segment
Of blackly shining asphalt
With the wiper moving across it
    Clearing, blurring, clearing.

But what to say of the road?
The monotony of its hardly
Visible camber, the mystery
    Of its far invisible margins,
Will these be always with us,
The night being broken only
By lights that pass or meet us
    From others in moving boxes?

Boxes of glass and water,
Upholstered, equipped with dials
Professing to tell the distance
    We have gone, the speed we are going,
But never a gauge or needle
To tell us where we are going

80

Or when day will come, supposing
   This road exists in daytime.

For now we cannot remember
Where we were when it was not
Night, when it was not raining,
   Before this car moved forward
And the wiper backward and forward
Lighting so little before us
Of a road that, crouching forward,
   We watch move always towards us,

Which through the tiny segment
Cleared and blurred by the wiper
Is sucked in under our wheels
   To be spewed behind us and lost
While we, dazzled by darkness,
Haul the black future towards us
Peeling the skin from our hands;
   And yet we hold the road.

I KNOW A MAN

As I sd to my friend, because I am
always talking,—John, I

sd, which was not his
name, the darkness sur-
rounds us, what

can we do against
it, or else, shall we &
why not, buy a goddamn big car,

drive, he sd, for
christ's sake, look
out where yr going.

   Not to say too much. MacNeice's management is nice, refined,
standard. But the Creeley poem suddenly calls the other poem into
question and answers it! It is the trait of Creeley's best work, as here,

that it makes us hold judgment in abeyance, makes it seem—as in fact it is—superfluous, irrelevant. The event is immediate and true. The speed that the abbreviated notation implies is wholly consistent with what is occurring: it is where it is at. Part of a dissolution, dissonance. Where MacNeice labors, filling, Creeley, even within the growing complexity and difficulty of the situation, where we join him, sings. How simple! And how movingly concentratedly profound! How that broken "sur-rounds" surrounds, the self-criticism and the grindingness of "because I am / always talking", the isolation and projection of "which was not his / name," or how it is the poet's "term" and ours, the excitement in the penultimate stanza and the sharp painful braking of the last, the urgency of it, the feeling of near disaster, throwing us back upon the futile wish of "a goddamn big car." The "goddamn" bringing us over to the weight of "for / christ's sake"—uncapitalized, nearer us by far. The colloquial registering at each point. Each syllable pulls its weight and no punch pulled. There isnt "time," least of all to embroider.

As later in "Anima Hominis" Yeats adds:

> . . . I think that we who are poets and artists, not
> being permitted to shoot beyond the tangible, must
> go from desire to weariness and so to desire again, and
> live but for the moment when vision comes to our
> weariness like terrible lightning, in the humility of
> the brutes . . .

Perhaps even truer (if true can be given degree) if the Yeatsian flamboyance is cut and found again, more illuminated, in Dante-Aristotle's:

> . . . For in every action what is principally intended
> by the doer, whether he acts of natural necessity or
> voluntarily, is the clarification of his own image.
> Thus is it that every doer, to the extent of his doing,
> delights in it, for everything that is desires its own
> being; and since in doing the doer's being is somehow
> amplified, delight necessarily follows . . . Nothing,
> therefore, acts unless it may thereby manifest what-
> ever it is . . .

To watch Creeley's mutations of what is to hand, or ear, is to see, to hear, how the inward draws to itself every possible (usually

82

subverted) relation, stratagem, to make fun of it, probe it, almost, as
in

WAIT FOR ME

give a man his
I said to her,

manliness: provide
what you want I

creature comfort
want only

for him and herself:
more so. You

preserve essential
think marriage is

hypocrisies—
everything?

in short, make a
Oh well,

home for herself.
I said.

And here's the model, Williams'

THE TESTAMENT OF PERPETUAL CHANGE

Mortal Prudence, handmaid of divine Providence
    Walgreen carries Culture to the West:
hath inscrutable reckoning with Fate and Fortune:
    At Cortez, Colorado the Indian prices
We sail a changeful sea through halcyon days and storm,
    a bottle of cheap perfume, furtively—
and when the ship laboreth, our stedfast purpose,
    but doesn't buy, while under my hotel window
trembles like as a compass in a binnacle.

83

a Radiance Rose spreads its shell—thin
Our stability is but balance, and wisdom lies
petals above the non-irrigated garden
in masterful administration of the unforeseen
among the unprotected desert foliage.

'Twas late in my long journey when I had clomb to where
Having returned from Mesa Verde, the ruins
the path was narrowing and the company few
of the Cliff Dwellers' palaces still in possession of my mind

The switch from WCW's historical shiftings with double ironies to the highly-charged personal, the relations almost invariably "screwed up" between a husband and wife, between Creeley and his lady, is characteristic. Yet I doubt if any poet has ever more doggedly explored the ramifications of what goes on between two human beings, presumably adult, who live under one roof, who sleep in or use one bed, or what does *not*. And the scrupulous examination he constantly subjects love/relation to. No longer "romantic" or not in any usual sense: the anti-heroic quotidian, but no less intense and joined for all that. Strindbergian.

To be in love is like going outside to see what kind of day

it is. Do not
mistake me. If you love

her how prove she
loves also, except that it

occurs, a remote chance on
which you stake

yourself? But barter for
the Indian was a means of sustenance.

There are records.

I think it is Valéry who emphasizes his delight in poetry pivots upon its "transitions," how thought—as language—in it "turns." In

Creeley what we would tend to call, if it were not inevitably jargon, the "intuitive" predominates. More than "thought" turns here: the movement worms its way forward through a logic of feeling rather than that specifically of thought, though it has seemed crucial to me that thought itself be recognized as feeling, and that feeling itself is a way of thinking, by no means "primitive," but clearly embodied. (Indeed, formal thought often has struck me as being as naïve as it is constipated by its adherence to set structures.) Anyhow, it is, when it works in Creeley, a source of astonishment and deep delight, to move with him, to feel the implication of risk (though the question seems to dawn only when "yourself" is put on the line) in love's open exchange and how risk *is,* clearly, what there is that sustains. The opening lines have Creeley's already remarked cryptic utterance, simple, so simple as to be startling, lost within event, and revealed wholly as the poem gradually opens and closes. To know, that is, where one is, by giving oneself to it, going out into, to see.

Creeley's wit, I might say in passing, is never quite lighthearted (as even his most positive statements imply doubts). It is not irrelevant that he called his early small collection of "light verse" a "Snarling Garland." A wryness persists, a taking oneself to task, an effort, difficult surely, to begin to laugh at oneself. Salutary, at any rate.

The tightness works its way out into an ever cleaner sense of economy, of form:

LA NOCHE (originally EL NOCHE, a slip)

In the court-
yard at midnight, at

midnight. The moon is
locked in itself, to

a man a
familiar thing.

Which bears odd resemblance to a haiku by Kikaku:

Locked & bolted
the castle gate
winter moon.

85

In the whimsicality of "Juggler's Thought" there is an underriding pathos, of lost Eden. And with the second section, 1956-58, come some of the unhappiest love poems of our time. As in the final stanzas of "A Form Of Woman":

My face is my own, I thought.
But you have seen it
turn into a thousand years.
I watched you cry.

I could not touch you.
I wanted very much to
touch you
but could not.

*(note the break between
"to" and "touch")*

If it is dark
when this is given to you,
have care for its content
when the moon shines.

My face is my own.
My hands are my own.
My mouth is my own
but I am not.

Moon, moon,
when you leave me alone
all the darkness is
an utter blackness,

a pit of fear,
a stench,
hands unreasonable
never to touch.

But I love you.
Do you love me.
What to say
when you see me.

86

In such poems it is amazing to see a man hold on, grip structure for salvation, making the rope while climbing it, for that is what one feels. Or even as Stevens put it, proven here, "the poem is the cry of its occasion."

Beyond the poems that mock romance:

> She walks in beauty like a lake
> and eats her steak
> with fork and knife
> and proves a proper wife . . .

or

> Out of the table endlessly rocking,
> sea-shells, and firm,
> I saw a face appear
> which called me dear . . . ,

where the frank burlesque/doggerel is used to bitter effect, the crisis is openly vented:

A MARRIAGE

> The first retainer
> he gave to her
> was a golden
> wedding ring.

> The second—late at night
> he woke up,
> leaned over on an elbow,
> and kissed her.

> The third and the last—
> he died with
> and gave up loving
> and lived with her.

It could hardly be more clinched and final (the reader interested can go to the intense prose of *The Island* for more detail). Gradually, however, he works his way out of that pit. And it may be said that in all this a too private despair is being displayed. And so it would be, and in many other instances is, if the poet were incapable of finding

87

the center of the experience, of saying it true, so that we know the pain only for what we feel, as the poet gives it to us, is lost, is a love.

Out of this despair comes more and more quietly again a singing. A belief. A strand. As at the end of "The Door":

> I will go to the garden.
> I will be a romantic. I will sell
> myself in hell,
> in heaven also I will be.
>
> In my mind I see the door,
> I see the sunlight before me across the floor
> beckon to me, as the Lady's skirt
> moves small beyond it.

At least there is a teasing saving presence of hope, grace, something (like fear?). What follows is lustration. Rhyme in water. Lucid dream.

> . . . God is no bone of whitened contention.
> God is no air, nor hair, is not
> a conclusive concluding
> to remote yearnings. He moves
>
> only as I move, you also move to
> the awakening, across long rows, of beds,
> stumble breathlessly, on leg pins and crutch,
> moving at all as all men, because you must.

Which suddenly sounds as though Stevens, playing Beckett, were addressing us.

In "The Rain," with its recollected music of Duncan's "O let me die, but if you love me, let me die," with its *Pervigilium Veneris* fragrance, the final two stanzas yearn for outwardness:

> Love, if you love me,
> lie next to me.
> Be for me, like rain,
> the getting out
>
> of the tiredness, the fatuousness, the semi-
> lust of intentional indifference.

88

Be wet
with a decent happiness.

It is both strength and weakness that when Creeley speaks we feel him personally present, an authentic personality, no persona, as against, say, Duncan of "The Albigeneses" I quoted, where the poet speaks in the role of "the poet." Creeley is up against it, wherever he is, we feel, and out of it emerges a voice, but transmuting harshness to intensity, intensity towards music, as poetry. The shapes of that poetry, the heart of his effort, seem to contradict his avantgardistic position, for they demonstrate a strict relation to the tradition of the lyrical quatrain. Of the final 38 poems in this collection; that is, his most recent work, only 3 are *not* in quatrains. Rhyme is always an immediate possibility, yet never anything but another sounding of edges, an adjunct to the total "ring" of the poem. A pulling in together of the music meaning engenders in language, felt meaning, meaning feeling for meaning. Or the poem dedicated to Louis Zukofsky,

THE HOUSE

Mud put
upon mud,
lifted
to make room,

house
a cave,
and
colder night.

To sleep
in, live in,
to come in
from heat,

all form derived
from kind,
built
with that in mind.

So much of this effort is one that brings poetry back to each of us as each. Not that the literary doesnt crop up, or lack for validity

89

anyhow, but that every poem is an occasion that one man came to comes to, finding for us, while finding himself, words for our occasion.

From here the act is, more even than Olson realizes in his "figure of outward," the primary one so easily lost sight of, so much again more difficult, the "major aim" of the poet as Zukofsky beautifully puts it:

> . . . not to show himself but that order
> that of itself can speak to all men.

Not that a man doesnt stand more and more revealed as his art discovers him in it, to others' eyes, but that personal private revelation must become each beholder's, listener's, partaker's, realization.

(from *Kulchur* No. 8, Winter 1962)

The Angel of Necessity

Letters of Wallace Stevens, selected and edited
by Holly Stevens (Alfred A Knopf, 1966)

> *To live in the world of creation—to get into it and stay in it—to frequent it and haunt it—to think intensely and fruitfully—to woo combinations and inspirations into being by a depth and continuity of attention and meditation—this is the only thing.*
>
> HENRY JAMES
> (quoted in *Letters of Wallace Stevens*, p. 506)

No poetry of the 20th century was less predictable than that of Wallace Stevens. It seems even yet like pure fluke. And of all the lives of the poets known to me none has struck me as being, outwardly at least, as unremarkable as that of Stevens. The *Letters* only reveal and confirm what the legend had indicated: that the legend is the poetry.

From Reading, Pa., to Hartford, Conn., that's about the size of it. The theory is simple enough, baldly stated: "I am what is around me." But wait a minute: "panache upon panache" deploys. Suddenly, out of the wilderness of the normal, of the ordinary, come these extraordinary celebrations of the actual, such fantasies of the spirit as make us quicken again to see what world it is we inhabit after all.

To read these letters is to have anyhow brought home decisively five points about the man and poet Wallace Stevens.

1. For the imaginative intelligence the ordinary is the most fertile source for whatever poetry extraordinary may occur.

2. An authentic voice will be pervasive and always integral.

3. The intimate discovers its maximal scope in supra-personal projections of its realizings.

4. Poetry is one of the sanctions of life.

5. The devotion to poetry is the devotion to whatever human community.

91

Let me examine each of these statements in the light of this correspondence and drawing upon whatever other evidences occur within the published work.

I.

For the imaginative intelligence the ordinary is the most fertile source for whatever poetry extraordinary may occur.

Even today there are countless people who scarcely wander far from their native ground. I recall a shopkeeper in Paris telling me that she had never been from her suburban arrondissement to the centre of the city. But to find a poet, and one of such decided scope as Stevens, who has rather early in his career settled down to a small city life is certainly odd. Stevens' eccentricity, if you will, resides in his very "normality."

He had done his do at Harvard—without overstaying it either, just long enough to have had contact with Santayana as a poet— pushed on, after some hesitation, through law school and then did a rough-and-ready tour of North America that had some repetition soon after in his early work with the insurance claims job he entered. So that his sense of the continent and his fondness for Florida was firsthand—though it was more eye than hand. But the bulk of his life was the routine that so many know these days: home to office and office to home. And he rarely digressed after his only child, the editor of this book, was born.

Independence is the virtue his old-fashioned Pennsylvania Dutch parents most inculcated, independence of language without loss of courtesy or care. At age 15 he could write to his mother:

> If Reading were as miserable as Ephrata I should be
> solaced in a measure but I can at least swim in clean,
> clear, wet water, I can eat food, I can swear when ever
> the eloquence of boiling passion rises, I can use both
> eyes when looking, I can contract debts, I can be your
> own dearest tootsey wootsey—.

That's 1895. From summer holiday home. Can anyone fail to feel the humor, the affection, the unusual language command already moving? And there is, moreover, a feeling of "pleasure" in handling language.

At no time in his life, so far as these letters disclose, and they are, if not exhaustive, very generous in their offerings and very openly edited—even possibly to the point of aching some, does Stevens bow to any man's opinion at the loss of his own. His own inimitable and indomitable nature procures its own responses.

The leverage is the actual, the so-called "real," the "necessary angel" he so often evokes. "For my own part," he writes in 1947, "I like to live in a classic atmosphere, full of my own gods and to be true to them until I have some better authority than a merely contrary opinion for not being true to them. We have all to learn to hold fast."

The stage is small, the circle of acquaintances small, but not constricting, somehow never constricting, more a constellation of such people as could share joys and pains of life with him upon an imaginative, not imaginary, level: someone in Ireland, someone in Cuba, someone in Ceylon, someone in Paris, his "agents."

A quiet life, then, a normal business at the office, gardening at home, an occasional trip to New York for shopping or to meet a friend or to see an exhibit at a museum or the Morgan Library. If he had enemies, they are not visible in the letters. He seems to have been friendly to a number of associates in law and insurance and been liked. And though he regretted that he couldnt devote all his energies to poetry, he as characteristically turned down the Norton Chair at Harvard, when it was belatedly offered him, for fear he might be forced—at age 75—only months before his death (of cancer)—to retire from the company!

By the time of *Harmonium*—and he was already well into his 40's—his parents and closest sister were dead. The need to address his life most responsibly to wife and child undoubtedly accounts for his apparent dereliction of poetry for nearly a decade. There was also a virtual critical silence to *Harmonium*.

Even so, there is a natural reticence that haunts these letters and the poetry. It suggests the sanctity of the home, of the intimate. And the only signs of it in this book are the journal notes and the early letters to his wife. In large measure, the unspoken is a part of his eloquence.

The visible existence hinged upon making a good living, but no more accoutrements of the good life than books, a phonograph, a roomy house. No car. Hand-tailored clothes. As local in his loyalties as Dr. Williams, not so far away in Rutherford, was too. And yet the contrast between these old acquaintances presents part of the range in American literary perspective. The general practitioner naturally had a long direct relation to a large segment of his community and at a lower economic level, a life that had barer aspects. It needed a more expostulatory, immediate poetry. Stevens, more reserved and isolate within the community, turned instinctively to a poetry of reflectiveness, but with that dazzling breadth of imagination that draws everything to it and out.

So much is the savor of the immediate in nature or the exigencies of peace found in a house or a room at night. The simplest even occurs like a headline: "the sun comes up like news from Africa." No one has ever doted so much on picture postcards or found so much in them. His imagination took off at the meagrest hint—took off and yet never lost footing. The "reality principle" is the fundamental and recurring feature of Stevens' life and poetics.

He is our Wordsworth. The differences of our time are operative here in every sense. Meditations on the given proliferate into swarming extensions of possibility. The world is not distorted in Stevens' images, but it finds uncommon overlays until a fresh dimension of "reality" comes over us. It is as if we were newborn in the new light shed by this radiance:

> There were those that returned to hear him read from the
>   poem of life,
> Of the pans above the stove, the pots on the table, the tulips
>   among them.
> They were those that would have wept to step barefoot into
>   reality . . .

II.

An authentic voice will be pervasive and always integral. So it is with Stevens: he has peculiar presence. He is always distinguished. He has "style." And our natural curiosity to grasp how it is he came by it is, perhaps, reflected too in himself, in his preoccupation later in life with antecedents. It had no more desire to concoct a noble lineage than Shakespeare's appropriation of a family crest to set his father up by. But Stevens is explicit: (1945)

> . . . after muddling round with American genealogy
>   for several years, I think that a decent sort of car-
>   penter, or a really robust blacksmith, or a woman

capable of having eleven sons and of weaving their clothes and the blankets under which they slept, and so on, is certainly no less thrilling.

Part of the quest of ancestry, for the rooted, may also have been related to a dissatisfaction with the vagueness of the modern as against the sturdier reality of the past—or that possibility he could feel as an indigenous, if bare, poetry in Dutch Pennsylvania. It is never a matter merely of looking backward:

> (1948) . . . somehow, for all the newness in this world in which every familiar thing is being replaced by something unfamiliar, in which all the weak affect to be strong, and all the strong keep silence, one has a sense that the world was never less new than now, never more an affair of routine, never more mechanical and lacking any potency of fineness. Nicht wahr? It is as if modern art, modern letters, modern politics had at last demonstrated that they were merely diversions, merely things to be abandoned when the time came to pick up the ancient burden again and carry it on. What I mean is getting rid of all our horrid fiction and getting back to the realities of mankind.

The words find shape:

> These figures verdant with time's buried verdure
> Came paddling their canoes, a thousand thousand,
>
> Carrying such shapes, of such alleviation,
> That the beholder knew their subtle purpose,
>
> Knew well the shapes were the exactest shaping
> Of a vast people old in meditation . . .
>
> Under Tinicum or small Cohansey,
> The fathers of the makers may lie and weather.

For all his oddness or newness of speech, all his quirks, no poet of equal inventiveness has ever been less given to the eccentric as such. He laments punctuational deviations or typographical innovations. He likes clear sentence structure. None of this militates against a

95

thoroughgoing metaphorical renovation. After all, as he had written: "The world about us would be desolate except for the world within us" or, in another essay, of the imagination said: "It enables us to live our lives. We have it because we do not have enough without it." And this is elaborated—clinching the matter—into:

> When one's aunt in California writes that the geraniums are up to her second-story window, we soon have them running over the roof.

And so persuasive is Stevens' imagery, the irrepressible high spirits of it, we are egged on to question the trope by saying: Why should they run over the roof when they can come in at an open window and go out again at the open door? This is California.

Letters, essays, or poems, the voice is one and singular. The spirit is that of a man given the capacity of speech and the power to find in the simplicities of reality, or the superficial complexities of it these days, the grounds of a larger metaphormorphoses (!): nothing leaves off and nothing remains quite the same after he has touched it:

> The eye's plain version is a thing apart,
> The vulgate of experience. Of this,
> A few words, an and yet, and yet, and yet . . .

The first sounds of that "voice" we have come to know as true Stevens were in his collegiate journals and letters home and to his sweetheart and later wife. The marriage seems to have brought about a complete unity of poetry and voice, providing a confidence in walking about in the nakedness of one's inner being. As far back, or further, as 1900 we find the romantic utterance typically deflated by pinprick deprecation, the dread of being a poseur, the American scorn of effeminacy that dogs the notion of being a "poet" or "artist" and the sense of queerness:

> Sometimes I wish I wore no crown—that I trod on something thicker than air—that there were no robins, or peach dumplings, or violets in my world— that I was the proprietor of a patent medicine store—or manufactured pants for the trade—and that my name was Asa Snuff. But alas! the tormenting harmonies sweep around my hat, my bosom swells with "agonies and exultations"—and I pose.

In his essay "Two or Three Ideas" he has brought together the relation between personal tradition and style in a way that the letters continually exemplify as they keep modulating towards poetry:

> . . . We stand looking at a remembered habitation. All old dwelling-places are subjected to these transmogrifications and the experience of all of us includes a succession of old dwelling-places: abodes of the imagination, ancestral or memories of places that never existed. It is plain that when, in this world of weak feeling and blank thinking, in which we are face to face with the poem every moment of time, we encounter some integration of the poem that pierces and dazzles us, the effect is the effect of style and not of the poem itself or at least not of the poem alone . . .
>
> Style is not something applied. It is something inherent, something that permeates . . . It may be said to be a voice that is inevitable . . .

Style, as Olson puts it, "est verbum." And for verbal idiosyncrasy and command the USA has come up with no one quite the equal of Stevens. And it isnt the business of a Mark Twain or a Walt Whitman; that is, one determined to be an American type or archetype. He is as unpredictable as they were predictable. His use of French—or law Latin—is no affectation—no man, as his letters constantly show, was charier of the "act"—but what he felt was part of the language he was native to—and often the French words are left—at his own instance—unitalicized to indicate as much. His neologisms may not be available to others, but they well up and work perfectly in their contexts—like whoops of delight—and seem much less "devised" than the devices of a Cummings. Perhaps it all rises from "tedium vitæ," as suggested in this letter of 1954:

> . . . What profound grace it is to have a destiny no matter what it is, even the destiny of the postman going the rounds and of the bus-driver driving the bus. Well, one prizes this destiny most particularly when the wind is blowing from the north-north-east and when the great clock in the office hall, which ordinarily tells the time so drearily that it would take

twelve musicians to mark the true tediousness of it—sos-tenuto something, rings, with the same bells, periods that are all chiming gaiety . . .

It all ties in with the singularity any life must be, though few fully realize—both in the differences and in the relations those differences renew. In 1948, to another friend, touching also the ending of a year, rings a bell here:

> . . . One of the great spectacles in the world today is the flood of books coming from nothing and going back to nothing. This is due in part to the subjection of literature to money, in part to the existence of a lettered class to which literature as a weapon just does not exist. Literature nowadays is largely about nothing by nobodies. Is it not so? What kind of book would that dazzling human animal Consuelo sit down to read after she had finished washing blood off her hands and had hidden once more her machete in the piano? Will you write it for her? Sartre or Camus would if they had time.
>
> These stimulating suggestions are most inappropriate to the month of Christmas. Perhaps they are part of the revulsion I feel after looking through the book catalogues that have been coming in. Here one is in a fury to understand and to participate and one realizes that if there is anything to understand and if there is anything in which to participate one will pretty nearly have to make it oneself. Thus José stands up in his room at 2 Dickinson (as the clock strikes midnight and as Eliot and Blackmur step into their nightshirts and kneel down to say their prayers) and he creates—by mere will a total wakefulness, brilliant in appearance, multi-colored, of which he is the dominant master and which he fills with words of understanding. Well, if he doesn't do it at 2 Dickinson, he may do it somewhere else. Bárbaro! Here the word shows its excellence. I suppose one never really writes about life when it is someone else's life, in the feeble laborious reportage of the student and artist. One writes about it when it is one's own life provided one is a good barbarian, a true Cuban, or a true

Pennsylvania Dutchman, in the linguistics of that soul which propriety, like another Consuelo, has converted into nothingness.

Or more briefly as it finds voice in poetry:

One poem proves another and the whole,
For the clairvoyant men that need no proof:
The lover, the believer and the poet.
Their words are chosen out of their desire,
The joy of language, when it is themselves.

III.

The intimate discovers its maximal scope in suprapersonal projections of its realizings.

To read a man's letters—realizing that much or most of it was not intended or expected to be read by others or the one other addressed—is to feel, so close is the life yet involved here, like a professional eavesdropper. In any case, the respect and feeling we have for the dead can only be measured by the respect and feeling we have for one another in our lives.

There is nothing in these letters we need for reading the work he had already generously provided. Yet it is only human—and not in the worst way—to be glad that they are available, even as a super-fluity. Think how great an event it would be for the human spirit if, suddenly, a hundred letters written by Shakespeare throughout his life and touching his daily existence and work should be discovered and shared with us. Beyond explications, the poetry itself would at once share in the new "light" by wanting to be read with such "knowledge" in mind. It would be as exciting as the discovery of another Sumeria before Sumeria.

The fact that Stevens was a "loner" only enhances one's desire to know more what moved within him, to grasp the springs—as I have said—of his imagination. This isolation, though not that of a hermit by any means, was of an order that should, by all odds, have produced a provincial or a dude dandy—and perhaps to some that is what he seems. Yet it is Hart Crane, who scoured the literary society of his time, who is the dude and the provincial. Nor is it merely a matter of higher education in Stevens' case. There is a magnitude of vision and a maturity of judgment at work.

His metaphorical epiphanies are never rhapsodies in blue. Indeed, "The Man with the Blue Guitar" invariably suggests the many-faceted sensibility of a Picasso with its imaginative penetration and afflatus. He was as well read as any of his contemporaries and in his modest way remained vigorously aware of painting and sculpture and music. He travelled only "at home," but wrote of Paris as if he were an exile from it. He has none of the pedantry or pretentiousness of Ezra and his literary circle ended at his doorstep. The language of imagination, extended from the realization so tellingly put—

> The poem is the cry of its occasion,
> Part of the res itself and not about.
> The poet speaks the poem as it is,
>
> Not as it was: part of the reverberation
> Of a windy night as it is, when the marble statues
> Are like newspapers blown by the wind. He speaks
>
> By sight and insight as they are. There is no
> Tomorrow for him. The wind will have passed by,
> The statues will have gone back to be things about.
>
> The mobile and the immobile flickering
> In the area between is and was are leaves,
> Leaves burnished in autumnal burnished trees
>
> And leaves in whirlings in the gutters, whirlings
> Around and away, resembling the presence of thought,
> Resembling the presences of thoughts, as if,
>
> In the end, in the whole psychology, the self,
> The town, the weather, in a casual litter,
> Together, said words of the world are the life of the world.

—this is his language, his persuasion.

He is utterly American. You have only to think of him in relation to Valéry, with whom he is often compared in his meditative approach and in his concern with a poetry of poetry. Stevens has nothing of Valéry's polish or classicism. Stevens could relish the annual Harvard—Yale football classic and that's about as far in that direction as he was likely to go. And nothing would have been more distasteful to the Frenchman, we may be sure. Stevens was "normal" with a vengeance, home-made, but not sentimental or stuffy. Valéry approached poetry as if it were a mathematical problem demanding a pure solution—as an equation. This has its interest too, but it is not what Stevens was at. He wanted to give pleasure and to offer a poetry that could realize life more fully at a time when so much of the traditional has gone by the boards.

The movement from the home, the quotidian, to the universal, beyond mere private confession or autotherapeutics, was an immediate instinct of his, as in an image from a typical Sunday walk of his in the years before his marriage in New York (1909):

> [to his fiancée] . . . almost a September sun (I know them all)—when the earth seems cool and the warmth falls like a steady beam . . . The woods along the side of the road looked at their height. And yet at twilight, in the neutral light, as I looked over the edge, I observed, meekly, that what I had thought to be various shades of green, were, indubitably, green and brown and yellow—oh, the faintest brown and the faintest yellow, yet brown and unquestioned yellow. You see!—I did not altogether respond—my sensibilities were numb—emotion sealed up. It is true. —But when the sun had set and the evening star was twinkling in the orange sky, I passed a camp—where gypsies used to camp years ago. There were two or three campfires and at one they were broiling ham. Well . . . I did respond to that sugarey fragrance—sensibilities stirred, emotions leapt— . . . It was worthwhile, by Jupiter! Not that I give a hang for ham—horrid stuff. But it was the odor of meat—the wildness or the sense of wildness . . . I am glad I passed the camp—and I am glad they were not eating boiled potatoes . . .

It is the same urge that senses

> The way, when we climb a mountain,
> Vermont throws itself together.

Or earlier and always, in "Sunday Morning" when the daily exotica and the remote transfiguration of an ancient idea—

Complacencies of the peignoir, and late
Coffee and oranges in a sunny chair,
And the green freedom of a cockatoo
Upon a rug mingle to dissipate
The holy hush of ancient sacrifice . . .

—attain to the simple grace of the natural scene in

She says, "I am content when wakened birds,
Before they fly, test the reality
Of misty fields, by their sweet questionings . . ."

and find their natural and universal orbit in

Deer walk upon our mountains, and the quail
Whistle about us their spontaneous cries;
Sweet berries ripen in the wilderness;
And, in the isolation of the sky,
At evening, casual flocks of pigeons make
Ambiguous undulations as they sink,
Downward to darkness, on extended wings.

How often do we find such words completing us and in a faith
we have no time to question? And the hint of that final image in the
merest word of a letter of a Sunday morning of May 1909:

Today I have been roaming about town. In the morning I walked down-town—stopping once to watch
three flocks of pigeons circling in the sky. I dropped
into St. John's chapel an hour before the service and
sat in the last pew and looked around. It happens that
last night at the Library I read a life of Jesus . . .

More and more, as the life went on and the years bent in, as both
poems and letters reiterate, the actual seized him by its "essential
bareness." As in the "scrawny cry" of an unknown bird

. . . at daylight or before,
In the early March wind.

How the letters protest against age, against the finality of being
"collected." And now every detail, mortal and momentary, takes on
immensity without losing proportion, as in 1952:

This morning I walked around in the park here for
almost an hour before coming to the office and felt as

102

blank as one of the ponds which in the weather at this time of year [October] are motionless. But perhaps it was the blankness that made me enjoy it so much . . .

Lebensweisheitspielerei.

> Weaker and weaker, the sunlight falls
> In the afternoon. The proud and the strong
> Have departed.
>
> Those that are left are the unaccomplished,
> The finally human,
> Natives of a dwindled sphere . . .
>
> Each person completely touches us
> With what he is and as he is,
> In the stale grandeur of annihilation.

As he could say in a letter of Marianne Moore, whom he always enjoyed and admired (1952):

> . . . She belongs to an older and much more personal world: the world of closer, human intimacies which existed when you and I were young—from which she and her brother have been extruded like lost sheep. As a matter of nature they stick together. What she has she has tried to make perfect. The truth is that I am much moved by what she is going through. It is easy to say that Marianne, the human being, does not concern us. *Mais, mon Dieu,* it is what concerns us most.

The maturing poetry is the maturing life. The movement between metaphor and meaning reduces to the one true voice, never closer to us and never allowing for our motions more, no longer adducing anything that is not wholly felt and realized:

> The way the earliest single light in the evening sky, in
> spring,
> Creates a fresh universe out of nothingness by adding itself,
> The way a look or a touch reveals its unexpected magnitudes.

IV.

Poetry—in his own words—is "one of the sanctions of life."

Needless, perhaps, to say, all the points that I am making in this essay are indivisible and only some of the ways of seeing the life and work of a man of supreme imagination into "ideas" that remain forceful and vital. For all the finality of life and the gestures we make, there is never an end, only ends we let ourselves accept for lack of sufficient openness.

Poetry opens wider.

He read rarely in public and just as rarely, it would appear, in private—aloud. The poems are silent conversations, the life of the mind rooted in the life of the feelings and in natural occasion. He can argue against large audiences, but he is not quite convincing, for we hear of his pleasure in a late letter at the full house he found himself addressing at the Y in New York. Nevertheless, in a letter of 1948, in recoiling from the audience he scarcely knew, he declares himself:

> . . . Your question about the audience for whom I
> write is very much like the question that was asked of
> a man as to whether he had stopped beating his wife.
> But, as it happens, I know exactly why I write poetry
> and it is not for an audience. I write it because for me
> it is one of the sanctions of life. This is a very serious
> thing to say at this time of the morning, so I shall let
> it go at that for the moment.

He was very much "a man who needed what he had created"—which sounds like a variation on an Hasidic tale told by Martin Buber: "Rabbi Mikhal once said to his sons: 'My life was blessed in that I never needed anything until I had it.'"

Despite the apparent rejection of an audience, there can be no mistaking Stevens when he states that poetry must give pleasure. No poetry has ever been made, or ever will be, that does not wait upon others. The approbation and confirmation of life intended by the word "sanction" turns upon art's public act, though performed in the sanctuary of the individual. Art is not cult, though it may be cultured. It is realization given its most accessible presentation.

Stevens likes his fruit to come "popped with juice" to the table.

He is anything but dry—even when abstruse. He is the possessor of a spontaneous and free-swinging imagination that manages, even so, a remarkable accuracy and discipline. He writes, prose or poetry, with relish. Analogy follows analogy, metaphors multiply, language flares and grows large with meaning—and then grows small again—decisively—until one wonders with him, towards the close of a life (and is one ever anywhere else?) if it hasnt all been "a skeleton's life":

> . . . nothing has been changed except what is
> Unreal, as if nothing had been changed at all.

And yet, unlike the determined glumness of Beckett's intellectual dead-end-ry, Stevens sees the cheer of lucidity, of "things as they are" as sufficient "glory" against the waywardness of destiny and the dark night. As a note to Delmore Schwartz in 1950 informs us:

> . . . You are fascinated by evil. I cannot see that this
> fascination has anything on the fascination of good. A
> bird singing in the sun is the same as a dog barking in
> the dark.

Not that it doesnt hurt as much as any, or feel the imminences: (about a year before his death)

> We remain quietly at home, engaged in meditation
> and prayer and thoughts of Paris. I have been trying
> to do a few poems. Just as one experiences the world
> in terms of one's age and physical condition, so one
> experiences poetry, I am afraid, in the same terms.
> The feelings, the great source of poetry, become
> largely the feeling of & desire to sit under the trees on
> a bench in the park . . .

And the poems enter:

> It is an illusion that we were ever alive . . .

or:

> It makes so little difference, at so much more
> Than seventy, where one looks, one has been there before . . .

Out of the drab, however, out of the least, out of a life trued by the local, by feeling and intelligence, he realized a poetry that sounds even in the letters a joyous recognition of relation. He writes at the

105

edge of poetry at all times, as if that sanction poetry gives to life was his to give in response to others. So that his letters open often with such instinct to communicate pleasure received, as if sharing his own poetic capacity as a common capacity:

> I am like a man wandering in a desert, and your letters are like visions of someone carrying water in my direction . . .

> One of the brightest things about Ceylon—Dominion or no Dominion—is that it contains at least one human being who is willing to take a lot of trouble to give other people pleasure . . .

> I am glad to hear you are only half dead . . .

> The weather has been so rotten that I am finally driven to writing to my friends in order to cheer myself up . . .

> Your *Alegres Pascuas* greeting was like a wand: a diversion from the normality of the normal . . .

> Coming into the office this morning and finding your letter on top of the mail was like walking out of the mist into a cheerful and friendly room . . .

Perhaps these minor words, these words *en passant* reveal why there is life for us in the poetry too. These are not just so many gambits. He is writing to those who are "with" him. But the role of poet is operative in the least moment. The life it sanctions in him he must try to extend for others. The kindness and gentleness and sparkle of the spirit at work here, even clearly against the moment's mood, are moving testimony to a "good man."

Not that he isnt frank to the point of bluntness, for poetry—of all fine art—insofar as it is a sanction of life—is demanding and cannot be dodged. And it is not a question here of whether one agrees with his opinions or not; they are all thoughtful, genuine, and delivered in good faith. So he can write of a book by Bryher, whom he knew, in 1952:

She is sentimental: not crudely so, but delicately, obscurely: yet all the same sentimental. The very subject of the book is a sentimental subject. It is something reflected, not lived, and that is why it is so difficult to become really absorbed in it . . .

He would not defend Pound, though it was the "thing" to do at the height of the Bollingen controversy, for he felt lack of competence to do so:

I don't suppose there is the slightest doubt that he did what he is said to have done. While he may have many excuses, I must say that I don't consider the fact that he is a man of genius as an excuse. Surely, such men are subject to the common disciplines . . .

but he mitigates this sensibly by adding:

. . . I don't believe that the law of treason should apply to chatter on the radio when it is recognizably chatter.

And he likewise felt no qualms at refusing a request to take part in a memorial of Dylan Thomas, referring to the silliness of Thomas's behavior in America, while also recognizing the tragedy of the loss.

There is a toughness in the man, which makes his feelings all the firmer when they turn up. And his criticisms of others in the arts reveal the faculties he brought to bear on his own work, the responsibility art implies:

[1945] . . . Caillois is provocative, but he is also provoking; he is not a man with a first-class mind, nor even with a good mind. He says something that is untrue and then makes a great point of proving that it is untrue. This is a very easy thing to do; the good thinker says that something is true and then proves that it is true; this is not nearly so easy . . .

[or in 1943] . . . It may be only too true that Van Gogh had fortuitous assistance in the mastery of reality. But he mastered it, no matter how. And that is so often what one wants to do in poetry: to seize the whole mass of everything and squeeze it, and make it one's own.

The preoccupation with the art reflects the attitude he has towards his calling. Just as he could criticize, he could also assist unstintingly, as in a recommendation for a Guggenheim candidate in 1955:

> . . . I don't suppose that a poet could ever maintain himself purely as a poet. To make it possible for an exceptional man at least to approach an existence as a poet, in which the question of maintenance is a subordinate problem, goes far beyond an award to promote or foster a desirable project, since the effect of it is to create a character wholly missing from contemporary literature . . .

Or again:

> poetry is not a literary activity: it is a vital activity . . . The good writers are the good thinkers. They are not able and skillful ink-slingers but people who put all that they have into what they say in writing.

For a man for whom poetry is one of the sanctions of life it is not surprising to find a lack of gossip in the letters. Contentiousness and pretentiousness are absent. He is professional, confident, persuasive, personal to the point of intimacy, but never private. Everything comes home, everything is imbued with poetry, everything finds just word. It is something more than a "supreme fiction": it is a life made true within the truest word.

From the earliest letters the capacity to project deepest response is found. The tender and charming fable he composed of the two pigeons for his future bride presages the late poem "Song of Fixed Accord," as well as others. Indeed, how many poems startlingly turn up at this time that only much later came to poem. Compare "Prologues to What is Possible" (1952)—

> There was an ease of mind that was like being alone in a boat at sea,
> A boat carried forward by waves resembling the bright backs of rowers

(and the images of Ulysses returning homeward to Penelope take on fresh charge and depth of meaning as Stevens' life comes round)—with:

108

The verse that you sent was perplexing. Just what was it that was discovered? But the mental scene of many rowers at sea at night lit by a starry flash was suited to remembrance. I say it priggishly—words have that faculty—And as a mental scene, aside from remembrance, the verse had its value.— From one of many possible figures—regard the mind as a motionless sea, as it is often. Let one round wave surge through it mystically—one mystical mental scene—one image. Then see it in abundant undulation, incessant motion—unbroken succession of scenes, say. —I indulge in heavenly psychology—I lie back and drown in the deluge. The mind rolls as the sea rolls.

Over and over again, tirelessly, as the poetry itself, sustaining itself upon itself, life sanctioned by life, the letters extemporize on the theme: whatever I am or may be is poetry and whatever honors man most truly is poetry. The rock is immediacy, the light imagination. To refresh and reenable each other to the necessary zest to care to continue.

Throughout the letters, throughout, in short, the life, integrity of vision is manifest. The aches are not transcended, they are transfigured. Hard not to see the "fatality" given a poet of "seeing things too well":

[1943] When I look at the pictures of the children and then consider that I am able to think of their lives as wholes, the thing becomes disturbing. It is like standing by and watching people come into the world, live for a while and then go out of it again. It isn't that it makes me feel old, because I don't feel old; I feel young. And it isn't that I think of all these lives as having ended before they had really matured. It just upsets me; I have not thought about it long enough to know why . . .

Which turns into:

There is so little that is close and warm.
It is as if we were never children . . .

109

No poetry is better than its maker. The quality of the life is the quality of the poetry—at best. Stevens' work is the epitome of a life of solitudes and solicitudes, the letters tell us, a life of rectitude and graciousness, of friends few but valued, of wit and grit, a man devoted to what he held dear, modest of realm but within his scope munificent: shades of the old "emperor of ice-cream." "A Child Asleep in its own Life" comes back to us and a passing comment in a letter of 1952 about the Rosencavalier: "The glancing chords haunt me and sometimes I try to reproduce the effect of them in words":

> Among the old men that you know,
> There is one, unnamed, that broods
> On all the rest, in heavy thought.
>
> They are nothing, except in the universe
> Of that single mind. He regards them
> Outwardly and knows them inwardly
>
> The sole emperor of what they are,
> Distant, yet close enough to wake
> The chords above your bed tonight.

V.

The devotion to poetry is the devotion to whatever human community. This takes us back to the ordinary never failing its extraordinariness, the realization that each life is a wonder and a wonder to be shared in such a way that it may be nourishing, pleasing, satisfying, stimulating.

Way back when, in his wanderings around New York, Stevens happened to be at hand to observe the obsequies of Stephen Crane and was appalled by the shabbiness of response on the part of the citizenry to one of its "heroes." The theme recurs in 1948:

> Conceding that Yeats was a man of world-wide fame,
> it is an extraordinary thing in the modern world to
> find any poet being so honored. Yet the funeral of
> Paul Valéry was a great affair. Moreover, people are as
> much interested in Rilke as if he was human enough

110

and in addition, something more. The fact must be that the meaning of the poet as a figure in society is a precious meaning to those for whom it has any meaning at all.

This recalls to me, when living in Paris in 1955, a bitter cold winter's day with a long slow line of people waiting to see the body of Paul Claudel in state at Notre-Dame. This simply hasn't happened ever in the United States and is unlikely ever to happen. The poet's dedication in America is, of necessity, different from its counterpart in Europe or the Orient. Stevens' determination to be "normal" implies a desire to be a poet *inside* society—and in this he correlates with Dr. Williams.

This concern of his with poetry as a central concern of human possibility is expressed in his idea of a Chair of Poetry at some key American university—a project he contemplated chiefly with the would-be benefactor of such a post, Henry Church, to whom the "Notes Towards a Supreme Fiction" is dedicated. In his memorandum to Church about the nature of the poet he affirmed:

> The knowledge of poetry is a part of philosophy and a part of science; the import of poetry is the import of the spirit. The figures of the essential poets should be spiritual figures. The comedy of life or the tragedy of life as the material of an art, and the mold of life as the object of its creation are contemplated . . .

The man of words comes forth, not simply for an honorary degree or self-seeking status, but for the dignity of all men inherent in all art. He addresses an audience of silences, not having to raise his voice from its inmost being, letting the words and the feeling realized in them hold whatever sway. And because he is a listener to silences, he learns to elicit from them kindred intelligences.

> . . . a poem must have a peculiarity, as if it was the momentarily complete idiom of that which prompts it, even if that which prompts it is the vaguest emotion. This character seems to be one of the consequences of concentration . .

> . . . for me the most important thing is to realize poetry . . . It is simply the desire to contain the world wholly within one's own perception of it. As it

111

happens, in my own case, and probably in yours, within perceptions that include perceptions that are pleasant . . .

. . . I write poetry because it is part of my piety: because, for me, it is the good of life, and I don't intend to lift a finger to advance my interest, because I don't want to think of poetry that way.

It is not a matter of "pure" poetry, though Stevens might not balk at that, nor is it quite the matter of "escape" that he at times promulgates, unless it be an escape into reality, into the feeling of being in all the fulness of human being. The very desire to comprehend the whole undermines any notion of a world apart. At the same time he recognizes the poem's own integrity, as *the* deposit and fund of human capacity:

. . . your remark that the final authority is always the poet is one of the things that I am given to contradicting. The final authority is the poem itself . . . The basis of Criticism is the work, not the hidden intention of the writer.

[1950] . . . Of course, I have had a happy and well-kept life. But I have not even begun to touch the spheres within spheres that might have been possible if, instead of devoting the principal amount of my time to making a living, I had devoted it to thought and poetry. Certainly it is as true as it ever was that whatever means most to one should receive all of one's time and that has not been true in my case . . .

[1951] Isn't it the function of every poet, instead of repeating what has been said before, however skillfully he may be able to do that, to take his station in the midst of the circumstances in which people actually live and to endeavor to give them, as well as himself, the poetry that they need in those very circumstances?

Earlier, in answer to a question, he had said:

> . . . The role of the poet today may be fixed by
> contrasting it to that of the politician. The poet
> absorbs the general life: the public life. The politician
> is absorbed by it. The poet is individual. The politi-
> cian is general. It is the personal in the poet that is the
> origin of his poetry. If this is true respecting the
> relation of the poet to the public life and respecting
> the origin of his poetry, it follows that the first phase
> of his problem is himself.
>
> This does not mean that he is a private figure. On
> the other hand, it does mean that he must not allow
> himself to be absorbed as the politician is absorbed.
> He must remain individual. As individual he must
> remain free. The politician expects everyone to be
> absorbed as he himself is absorbed. This expectation
> is part of the sabotage of the individual. The second
> phase of the poet's problem, then, is to maintain his
> freedom, the only condition in which he can hope to
> produce significant poetry.
>
> If people are to become dependent on poetry for
> any of the fundamental satisfactions, poetry must
> have an increasingly intellectual scope and power.
> This is a time for the highest poetry. We never
> understood the world less than we do now nor, as we
> understand it, liked it less. We never wanted to
> understand it more or needed to like it more. These
> are the intense compulsions that challenge the poet as
> the appreciatory creator of values and beliefs . . .

Stevens may address himself to an élite, but it is not an élite with class
concerns, but rather one that cuts through all such formalism. The
élite he addresses is that which any person may come to insofar as he
has desire and capacity to come to it. It is one of intellectual depth and
spiritual scope.

At the end of his life, after Yale University had decided to confer
a degree upon him, his state passed a resolution acclaiming him for
his poetic service and he answered it by saying:

. . . Such a resolution may be regarded as a way of
saying that in a state like Connecticut poetry is
recognized as an element of the life of the community
and this is all that a poet could ask for.

Perhaps it is wishful thinking on the part of any American poet
to say such things, seeing things as they are, but the hope is solid
enough—like the star on Marianne's steeple.

Other poets have done and will do other things, but no other
would or could have made an *œuvre* of such incomparable delight and
astonishment, transmuting and clarifying the terms of our quotidian
world. One can envy those who have yet to find him and at the same
time know that the poetry, like any living body, remains alive to
continual discovery. It is a poetry we could not have imagined having
and yet once having it, cannot imagine ourselves ever doing without.
It is one of the accesses of the recent intelligence of being human.
It is proof of imagination's community; as such is is a "constant
sacrament of praise."

Epilogue

The pensive man . . . He sees that eagle float
For which the intricate Alps are a single nest.

These letters we cling to—like Rilke's dying man turning back
for a last look at the mountains fading behind or beyond. It is like
waving adieu adieu adieu to one who is and is to be part of the house in
which we dwell, the spirit's abode and as no less intimate part of the
physical being we hold a little while and behold.

More than as a mine then for scholars, we have a sense of the man
of the poetry still intricate in the make of it. Of such souls we cannot
have enough. Here he is for us his most particular self arrayed in
poetry: the gay man, the sad man, the ordinary man in glittering
sombrero, the real man full of hexes, the unreal man brimming
hallucinations of the actual, and the candle he keeps bearing to us in
this space of a dark (if not darkest) night:

Within its vital boundary, in the mind.
We say God and the imagination are one . . .
How high that highest candle lights the dark.

Out of this same light, out of the central mind,
We make a dwelling in the evening air,
In which being there together is enough.

This figure moves almost without motion, vivid, illuminate, moving us before we know what is happening until we know ourselves willing captives of event—a figure of "words virile with his breath"—who can say and so does:

> *Inexplicable sister of the Minotaur, enigma and mask, although I am part of what is real, hear me and recognize me as part of the unreal. I am the truth but the truth of that imagination of life in which with unfamiliar motion and manner you guide me in those exchanges of speech in which your words are mine, mine yours.*

Here in the letters, but beyond them, in the poetry, in "the flawed words and stubborn sounds" is one Pennsylvania Dutch Connecticut Yankee member of the most durable of American heritages, its 20th century poetry, in his own guise now, the angel of necessity, in the light of the common place the uncommon spirit:

It is he, anew, in a freshened youth
And it is he in the substance of his region,
Wood of his forests and stone out of his fields
Or from under his mountains.

December 1966
(from *Caterpillar* I, October 1967)

115

Maximus Continuing

Charles Olson
Maximus Poems IV, V, VI (Cape Goliard / Grossman, 1968)

To resume:
>". . . the bow-sprit, the beak
>in, the bend is, in, goes in, the form
>that which you make, what holds, which is
>the law of object . . .
>
>call it a nest, around the head of, call it
>the next second
>
>. . . which you
>can do!"
>
>". . . :people
>
>don't change . . . only stand more
>revealed
>
>. . . know
>
>it is elements men stand in the midst of . . .
>
>. . . know polis
>
>not as localism . . .

root city . . ."

"the first human eyes to look again
at the start of human motion (just last week
300,000,000 years ago . . ."

" 'the people' (?!)—as though there were
anything/the equal of/
the context of/now!"

" . . . no hierarchies, no infinite, no such many
as mass, there are only
eyes in all heads,
to be looked out of"

" . . . so many, children,
who want to go back, who want to lie down
in Tiamat . . ."

"where my own house has been (where
I am
founded . . ."

"That a man's life
. . .
is what there is
that tradition is . . .

Historie

come bang into the midst of

our game!"

[the details set down
keeping the edge of
things acute/rough]

" . . . any of us
the center of a circle
our fingers
and our toes describe"

{Leonardo/Dürer}

renaissance

ON FIRST LOOKING OUT THROUGH JUAN DE LA COSA'S EYES

Passage to India: cod   God   fish

   "a Mud Bank"

"As dreams are, when the day
encompasses"

         "that we are only
         as we find out we are"

                           "that all start up
                           to the eye and soul
                           as though it had never
                           happened before"

"it better be, or
what's all this

for"

   "Out,
is the cry of a coat of wonder"

"When a man's coffin is the sea
the whole of creation shall come to his funeral"

         Gondwanaland

            coming back together

humpty dumpty
                    a moon's eyeview to prove it
                    anew

" . . . all things through all things,
. . . issues from the one"(Hesiod)

                    from Dogtown (Maximus):

a point of view we are stuck with:
            counting
                    towards
                        meaning:
a sense of what we are doing
of what is going on
where we are, or
have been

            the apparition comes again

Dogtown story/Merry's
marriage to myth
America/stars

already
busting out all over

hammering that rock

Olson: a sea of granite

desire

Who rages at the sell-out of his country
to account for it
for what it might have been, what was, what
may yet be

myth/god/miraculous

119

fact/act/being

death: Merry's/his

"Then only . . .
did the earth
let her robe
uncover and her part
take him in"

Information/siren song

to make it all cohere
coherent as it is

family

(sport: no evolution

neither turning back nor
advancing

uroboros/ouranos

dividing light and darkness god

He says

      BLACK "all the heavens,
          all few miles up"

        KNOWS better

        earth only
        stardistant
        in it

MAN/medusa/flower

light = carbon

de-composition

Duncan romping wordwise
opening up that "field

the first nine
to take it

the first scene

Going back always
to now

          "to the geography of it"

one of infinite centers

Fort Square

any man

Ol' son

     "skin

     plus this . . .

                    Polis

     is this"

Policing a beach/out of *Scientific American*
to be so gulled

(walking a winter day with me over rocks
 and back to house

quoting that

121

against his and my eyes
Or what words come to

between book ends

             Evangel/even angel
             wont do

Or it did

as we see/must

No race

and no trophies

earth
born to
to be borne to
to bear

and all that sky
cannot excuse heaven
as back parlor
the fast shuffle
immortal coil

     (the cat's deep growl
      more than points
      to speech

      my front garden
      comes up to my sill
      weeds

         like any flowers
      for and against
      the light

      to draw from nearer to

"The facts in the case are as described":

a likely story

like any myth

a likely story told often enough

inheres

       "down below"

                     uroboros/your motherfather

       "was the spirit of the mountain"

not any -ism/as soon as it becomes
that organ

listen to the vast inane

MAN

the
economy

no way to get around
as the sky does
earth

household (Gary picks from between teeth)

Of course it all works
if it is worked at

the strings
move/connecting

ideas

whose puppets
we play

divine man

figure him
out

"until the beast rises from the sea"

Proteus/Aphrodite

uroboros

THE ORIGINS & HISTORY OF CONSCIOUSNESS

coscienza/the new sigh-ends

"or Phryne (who's afraid of
walk into
the water"

Godtown USA: Ol' son stand Fortsquare
"a mother is a hard thing to get away from"

if that is what dying is supposed to be

born of

OF

but hard to get through to

to see/not stopping to

to breathe
all the way out

the loss of/absence of

"our love is for ourselves alone

I walk you paths of lives I'd share with
you simply to make evident the world
is an eternal event and this epoch solely
the decline of fishes . . . "

                                    no more "eternal"
that "infinite" (who has eyes, he said
beyond our circumscription
and our inscriptions
read:

        MAN
(no trespassing)
TO COME
A

        all dredged up/filleted
        and laid on the table

        facts/cooked

steeped in fire

Mnemosyne

                (counting from nine
                down—or is it from
                zero:

                        the numbers racket

                        greed/facts

"I'd like you to tell me what difference
you feel between man and statue, marble and
flesh."

"Not much. We make marble with our flesh,

125

and flesh with our marble."

"But one is not the other."

"As living force is not dead force."

Time. The degree of.

The place of
energy in

Where you break
into

continuing

          In ancient days
          existed
                    nothing . . .

          Ginnungagap

                         genug

satisfied?

No more than words are
with themselves

"the head of something"

          "the arms
          of Half Moon Beach
          the legs
          of the Cut"

                    Mammy!

Do we need to date it? As fresh as
the first man
dead

coscienza/co-scienza

His map

rounder and more
wrinkled

whiter and
more parched

mapunmaker of God'stown

fixed

on these pages

turning

away

    It is not easy/nor simple
    not to see

    feeling

and the facts
curtains up
reveal
a certain
play

    of the mind there is no end

    MAN

a way

out?

terms are
contra-

dictions

     "mocking bird"

" . . . she
felt she was her mother meaning my
body was hers . . ."

        uroboros

THE BEGINNINGS (Lord!
    capital gains
    a (THE) tradition

   " . . . hauled
    hair via hair rope
the statue into
place"

    "Come into this world":

past part/imperative

a reading

a yawning gulf

a well called Hvergelmir

"its accent is its own mirage"

"the Perfect Child"

      MAN

we know what to look for

lightyears

beyond a planting of the windless flag
MayJulypole
Tranquility

"the original unit
survives in . . .
                 salt"

                              empty pages
                              uroboros

coming out of it
going into

          "value received
               I herein testify"

                    (you too can see/listen)

the dream
          (Whitehead)
                         universe

as what is found out
within

the
economy

uroboros

          poeticks?

the making out the
discerning
               seeing is
beyond us
               transparent
self-effacing

129

distributing

as breath does

the air of
the air of

      "the Lady of Good Voyage"

"in the shape of a heart
. . . likewise new"

        "menhirs"

Stone hinge

"my memory is
the history of time"

         I mean
         we know what went on

         us

         you and me

". . . a mappemunde"
             (out of periplum)
" . . . to include my being"
             (wo den)
Peloria (dogdamned)

         "public figure better be
      what had he better be?"

        public

A giant: the first living creature

distinct and moral—as he says

" . . . open an opening
big enough for himself"

" . . . from Ma
                    x = i'm us
who is always there"

connecting the postman's truck
"at the corner of Rocky Neck Avenue

"north north west to Judas waters
home to the shore"

                "tesseræ"
                explicit

concerned with that literateness

connects "before"
with "after"
where we are

the other
another
now

        an underworld (gang)
        ferried via so much bull
        (imagine

        this

        "town

        placed as an island
        close to the shore"

A reader of Chronicles
making time ring
wringing time's make

the clock
makes
believe
          (to quote a one)

Sumatra/Java/South Pacific

X

yinyang
livingdying

why should we say/think
the dream ends
here

it is the well the water the egg
Okeanos

air:protein

the light house

" . . . reed-houses
on flooded marshes?"

(Speculations)

                images for imagists

There is no gist
no matter the
trice me gist us

LZ sees through
and brings back

into (a trice) quick

"I want that sense here, of this fellow
going home"

fear that runs to history
the documents
the signs of

life

It is begged conundrumed
made into
sense

      (no money in it
      to be sure

      an accounting

      public figure

      called for

      you

What do the gods mean

Who can we ask
but our selves

      "killed themselves
      against the lights between"

      too late
      soon enough

"beta'd"?

baited

Olson

>blanks (Ez the heathen Chinee)
>for the unknown
>time
>
>uroboros
>"entwined
>throughout
>the system"

gradually
the dream peers out

"the diadem of the Dog
which is morning
rattles again"

>>tincans
>>the sound of
>>marriage

of a city
a shore

foot and back

"the light hangs
from the wheel of heaven"

>>MAN

"the illusory
is real enough"

>>And the "real"
>>illusory enough?
"the suffering

is not suffered

the foreknowledge
is absolute"

CO-SCIENZA

livingdying
        "imagine the odor
which is true
at low-tide . . .
if you live . . . "

Asgard (shima) Midgard
to protect the world
from the world:

conclave/poetry

heaven (word)

transparent brilliancy

Mannus

McManus

MAN

US

OF

"Cunt Circle"

"the sea added"

a way to come in by
and be lost in the coming in by

a package: renaissance

chickenegg dumbcluck

OK
Have it your way
Be here

Charles Olson (that's a quote)
I believe
you

Can you
believe
that (this

Hansel & Gretel again
"and into the oven with her"

a history (ie?)

"published . . .
to make sure that what was known was
passed on to posterity . . ."
                              Vedic

the sounding of the sounds
enough

love never remembers
never forgets

"of land I am shod in,
my father's shoes"

the very next thing
after the rime dripped down
there solidified from it
the cow Authumla (Nurse)
from those teats spurted

four rivers of milk:

she fed Ymir.

Saint Sophia
herself our
Prayer
        Our
Lady of
Good (bon) Voyage

a little of this a
little of that it
circulates

uroboros

AGAIN:

"he who walks with his house on
. . . walks
with his house on his head"

" . . . fucked

by the Mountain

. . . how it was she was
so happy"

The Carmelite Lady Santayana recalled
who asked Are you happy? replied No—
but I am content.

" . . . the Virgin
held up
on the Bull's horns"

the lifting of siege of Orleans

The Duke of Alençon himself:

" . . . all in the straw together, and sometimes I
saw Joan prepare for the night (tu-whit tu-whoo)
and sometimes I looked at her breasts which
were beautiful, and yet I never had carnal
desire for her . . ."
                          The Puzzel. Not so: the
Duke. Raised/liberated—only to be burnt at
the stake, thereby hangs.
                          "to enter into their bodies"

What else is
fable is
life?

The name
we put to
it:

    "homo Anthropos"

    "The Cow
    of Dogtown"

the NEED to put it
in a sort of tough
vernacular:
                maximus

in the face of

MAN

    Dogtown Yucatan
    Ptah!

        The airs (Nut)
        of earth

138

               he allows
               Her

Paterkiller familiar ass
coming attractions:

ORPHEUS

Creeley's *Pieces?*

And this is where we've come to?

"at the boundary of the mighty world"?

no
contract

promise

quid pro quo (OK)

touring the world
tilling a small field
to its limits

And
beyond?

"It is Hell's mouth
where Dogtown ends

. . .
and it—this paved hole in the earth
is the end (boundary
Disappear."

               Another act
               "a century or so before 2000
               BC"

139

"the Stream, Tartarós
is beyond
the gods beyond hunger outside"

                    Okeanos
                    uroboros

                         X

no longer
straws
in the wind

bound

at center

a stool
a drum
a tent
Heaven & Earth

bound
Prometheus

center

burn

        MAN

house

        (OM)

            The way up
            The way down

strugglerepose

                    140

livingdying

inyo

meyou

Olson
Corman

a bond

"away from all the gods" (gauds)

"The life-giving earth"
The life giving earth

under
and over

"read your shadow slanted upward by your side, the tales
the tales to tell in the continuous speech . . . "

"the house I live in . . .
                              the door"

all that a woman can say
she does

                    "her Hill and place"

                    "the shape of light

        the lay,
                of flowers"

reticule
ridiculous

the wrinkles
at the eyes

the face
articulate
egg

    "the Head of the Maiden"

must one go back to

word

or

dragonseed

"dragon knows dragon"

word knows word

no promise

a present (a present indeed
intrudes

precludes

and so the future
haunts

    "it is the question of value
      which opens again"

Is "value" a question?

or one of the facts (acts
like love (he sd

to be dealt with

" . . . wrong"?

stupid

inescapably
so

   MAN

      "The total price"?
      Verdict

Judgement

on top of death
death

fucked by a Mountain

Virgin

          My father
          who had called this very maximus
          "Professor"
          and he balked

          until the old man said
          in answer

          "Because you look like one"

Seeing is

      what Olson isnt

but facts/by all means facts

as against
          "Between heaven and earth"

143

one
snow
mountain

unique
insistence

life's
necessitating
life

redundance

"I set out now

(entering white)

(the night of it)

in a box upon the sea"

But that he tries
to all that
small height
Maximus
claims

cares

and wants
care

6 September 1969
(from *Caterpillar 8/9*, October 1969)

Larry Eigner
Another Time in Fragments (Fulcrum Press, 1967)

In writing Larry a month or so ago about this most recent collection of
his work I said (more or less):

> There is often the unwritten poem behind the poem:
> a man tied, relatively, to one position, rather like a
> leashed dog (or cow, if you prefer), and gradually—
> trying to hold onto the visible and audible, the
> sensible and finally mental "world," a sort of a world
> anyhow—uncertain of more than the words, if
> words, of what gets put down and out. (So, in a sense,
> more Beckett than Beckett.)

In fact, as imitable as Larry's work tends to seem, it is decisively and
peculiarly marked by his own plight yielding its benefits—though it
rarely openly "bothers" to remark itself. And his hospital poems in
the latter section of the book are notable, in that respect: for what is
not said.

3

        and they all
            wave to me
        when I sit out there
        between their cars

This is an orientation that is hard at first, I imagine, for most readers to realize. The "me" is in his wheelchair on the street enjoying the sun and strictly confined openly to what everything offers as entertainment, as speculation, as wonderment, as source. To quote an older letter of mine, which someone else once quoted:

> Your poems are, I think, always "speculations" in the literal *and* figurative sense. Words are your safety pins. I feel as though you were hanging from a parachute held together by safety pins, the stork bringing its luggage to our chimneypots, or over the sea, not trying to get anywhere, a storm, a beach, a cloud to shore on, a grain of sand, or a tree whipped over a tilted roof.

That was, if memory serves me right, in relation to an earlier book, but the work—since the first poems appeared in *Origin* in 1954—is all of a piece, or pieces, and transparently so.

Larry generally seems to work off his typewriter on a single sheet of paper, sometimes on both sides, sometimes in margins, crowding more than one poem on a page, or more unusually on larger outsize sheets (devised or somehow come by), if my recall is accurate. (Most of his manuscripts have, often in carbons, come my way through the years and even yet.)

The random quality is often due to the brevity of the poet's attentions, acute and wandering. Finding every distraction a focal point and the alert mind mingling ideas, facts, as wires, hinges, bolts, and sometimes just flashes. Glimpses and glances, queer connections of the most familiar.

2

Again dawn

the sky   dropped
its invisible whiteness . . .

The switches are sudden, constant, unannounced and usually of a surprising freshness—but with no strain at shocking us:

5

wings fluttering up near the

146

> beginning of rain
>
>   I like to see
>   the pink car wet
>   wheels matched by a pool
>
>   the rain
>   muddy in sound . . .

As "easy" as it may seem, as it *is* (for him), it cannot be easily, if at all, by anyone else or anyone else's computer—precisely because it is true, it is the occasion of Larry rocking and rocked by his own quirky boat. The angle of his incidence touches coincidences in us, starts of awakenings, but the eyes are part of a quite clearly demarcated situation.

In a way what is *most* startling, at least to me, is the sanity of his vision, the straightness of it, which *may* be straitness. As if the strictness in this poetry were in the engrossment of the poet and that engrossment existential in the extreme.

Even in the final poem of uttered anguish, oddly enough, a certain directness of vision prevents expressionism from breaking in and introducing the grotesque:

> \# 141 (closing lines)
>
>   After trying my animal noise
>   i break out with a man's cry

I feel that the palsy that is his birthright and the highly developed intelligence and sensibility accompanying it have come to create a poetry of renewal, where nothing is taken for granted, nor is there a "structure" to be made or evaluated.

> The
> accidental/incidental
> enter into words as they fall,
> broach breath,
>   spasms perhaps
> poems:

147

chances
felt, weighed, loved
                    quietly
for what they *are* worth
pivoting upon the
immediate

His health is
that he restores to us
words in their spaces
                    the interventions
of language as perception,
event,
        occurrence

We cannot predict him
because he doesnt, cannot know either
        "what next?"
                    "how come?"—
what occurs to him
        to occur to us, to refer to us,
            to the poem, is
                            poem

The poems are entered upon the page
    in their own intrusion—so
            not constellated in a Mallarmean
                superbness
but no less extraordinary for
stamina, rightness, energy

coherent simply because they occur this way
        and are let be
        # 9

                    trail nest   upper tree

                remember
                and leave it   now   lie
                    beyond

                    clouds again   the
                    outline of peaks

                    those are the lakes

                    upon which the
                                    branches throve
                            tossed silence   shadows
                            descent from the wind

                    the area
                    is continuous   motors
                    are breathed on   books
                        change

The "play" in these pieces is everywhere, a dancing vision, where each thing, each word, is sensed, is seized, in a most particular geography, convergence of directions. As if the words spoke themselves towards us. And it may be this that makes in them, for me, a certain soundlessness, as if the words were uttered from the source of silence.

Some, if not all, have the quality that Ponge felt in writing his *Pine Woods Notebook* during the War in order to have something to read, to enjoy, to be at home with. And there is *that* that many poets I feel feel.

It is low-tension poetry, not written for critics, unmelodramatic and with a tendency disconcertingly in anthologies and periodicals to throw other works into curious relief, much as an Ozu film will make other films look phoney or pretentious by its undolled-up directness and clarity. Insight is always in sight: an action, not a report.

One perception moves upon another with that instantaneity Olson counselled in his *Projective Verse* essay and which Rimbaud had already picked up from Baudelaire at an earlier date. But there is none of the oratorical or the homiletical about Larry's poems, nor are they anecdotal; they are juggleries of language as perception, or perception perhaps as language, but beyond hope—or desire—of catching everything: letting the casual drop—or like fishing for minnows with a tennis net:

(from # 108)

the boundless closes in

In sum, the grace of one who sees what is given him, the inescapable that escapes by itself soon enough, and the givenness is present to him as it is present in its fulness, it would seem, to so few of us, and who can realize, has realized, here, something we may share:

133

Sometimes it's surprising how I don't think of death
  solid wall to eternity

    You stare and
  the sky is too little
    for the eye

          branches

        so is the color
        cars going by

    to that barrier
                  fingers
              to the lids of leaves
                  footbridges
              can look busy

              a stairway in a cottage
          burlapped bushes   fixed
                      dogs in the wind

              the dirt of clouds
              lifts through the seas

  Who will say this isnt love?

(from *Elizabeth* XIV: November 1969)

Philip Whalen
Severance Pay (Four Seasons Foundation, 1970)

The title, as the dedication to his godson explains, comes from an anecdote:

> One day something unexpectedly failed or bent;
> there was some small disappointment. Allen
> Ginsberg remarked,
> "Hmmmm. Not much severance pay in that, was
> there."

Phil—my nextdoor neighbor and friend—mostly makes poetry out of local deprecations—usually wired to explode in his own face—little detonations. A born executioner of the petty but irremediable self. 29 poems by my count: most quite short, the final "Birthday Poem"—17 pp.—out of the 51 of text.

American Chaplinesque: the poems deceptively easy; i.e., they work with more care and economy than immediately registers. And they live with a remarkable easy immediacy. References are close to home—some would say private and I cannot tell since I live too close to the man—but the particulars are clear and always given.

Phil has admitted that he is "addicted to books" and doesnt anticipate getting over such kicks. But what he quotes is what has struck him in one way or another and the "way" is the poem:

SOMETHING CHILDISH BUT
COMPLETELY CLASSICAL

Orpheus, Jesus, Osiris
All say: "Burst out of your tomb
And go on your way."

Serpent and plane tree
Holy and wise:
"We are immortal;
Only skin dies."

Phoenix entombed
In blazing pyre sings:
"Living or dying
All is bright fire."

The poems are each and all given their date of ascension. And
the dying implicit in the meaninglessness of any occasion tinges each
and all.

Phil is the comedian who always cries at his own jokes.

The too long to quote but lovely play of the poem dated-titled:
7:III:67 "O tell me it's only temporary" that freely diddles around
with the musical fissionability of surrealisms and ends up characteristically being turned off with:

> slide back just a little bit and let me
> quit it

to the ache of being hopelessly happy:

OCTOBER FOOD

Pine-tree child soaks in a teapot
Chrysanthemum perfume soup and a
Seasnail boiling in his shell, that I
May live forever.

Japanese twist to sentiment/sediment of Zukofsky.

Nobody could miss the appetite—the zest that consumes words
as food and food as language. And the peculiarly American tang—
nostalgic often—even when making fun of it—of "Bill Brown's
House In Bolinas":

Houses all scattered, all different, unrelated to the ground
or to each other except by road and waterpipe
Each person isolated, carefully watching for some guy
to make some funny move & then let him have it POW
Right on the beezer.

Unmuffled delight in speech, in petulance, in shit. The anger. The love that keeps creeping out—like nobody's dog in anyone's yard.

Playing Bach for himself and the passing neighbors, shrieking at the mongrel cats who bring in dirt while he vacuums the tatami or cursing the cat that bites (gratuitously) the foot of one who often does the feeding, the doors back and front open—letting the air flow through—at almost any hour. The cleanliness, the thoughtfulness, the daintiness of a bear of a man, beard of a man, who relishes whatever it is that it is to be:

25 : I : 68

Sadly unroll sleepingbag:

The missing lid for teapot!

As he says in "Walking Beside The Kamogawa . . .":

Suzuki Roshi said, "If I die, it's all right. If I should
live, it's all right. Sun-face Buddha, Moon-face Buddha."
Why do I always fall for that old line?

We don't treat each other any better. When will I
Stop writing it down.

And the opening line that follows on the next page of his "Birthday Poem":

Thank God, I don't have to write a poem . . .

But he does, of course—as Beckett's excuse for writing is simply that he does. As the self-denigration becomes everyman as everyday dying. An old rot. Which doesnt prevent someone who can talk, who finds curious satisfaction in it, from doing so.

The end of the same poem brings it back at a deeper pitch:

I'm always afraid you'll find out I love you
Then you'll hate me. How much does this matter, any more?

153

Two zeroes is one hundred.
Black to move and win.

Awake or asleep I live by the light of a hollow pearl

Once—about a year ago—at a party—Phil was given a big knife
to cut a cake baked for him—his birthday?—by my wife. As we all sat
solemnly joyful awaiting his work, he lifted the knife over his head as
if it were a samurai sword and brought it down with a resounding
blow through the heart of the sweet thing. We all awoke.

THE MADNESS OF SAUL

Everybody takes me too seriously.
Nobody believes anything I say.

(from *Elizabeth*: XVII, April 1971)

154

The Poetry of Lore

Gary Snyder
Regarding Wave (New Directions, 1970)

> **lore:** 1. *Archaic.* Act of teaching, or that which is taught; hence, instruction; wisdom; counsel. 2. Knowledge; learning; often, the whole body of knowledge possessed by a people or class, or pertaining to a particular subject, esp. when such knowledge is regarded as of a traditional description.
>
> *Webster's Collegiate Dictionary*

I take the book as it comes, from him, friend of the family—no need to go back to what went before, what stays of it, comes again through this. To be: here.

I think of Gary usually as in Kyoto, whether riding breakneck behind him on his motorcycle, embracing him, or eating with him at his place, looking for all the world like the first American ascetic, old young man from the mountains, something native to the earth, an animal child scampering up a tree, lookout for everyone below.

Now father, now builder of home, now husband, now maker of poem.

1.

Evangelist, rhapsodist, wordcrazed, thrown into and gathered again from things, coming alive anew to what there is, what he is, her:

WAVE

    Grooving clam shell,
        streakt through marble,
    sweeping down ponderosa pine bark-scale
        rip-cut tree grain
            sand-dunes, lava
            flow

    Wave   wife.

Characteristic is his use of slang/jargon, the most contemporary idiom, in an also accurate exact sense, as in "grooving" or in the next poem

SEED PODS

Seed pods seen inside while high.
trip of fingers
to the farthest limits of the thigh

where "high" and "trip" are given additional leverage.

Two strands intertwine: the ecstatic and the love of language, related to lore. The first reminds me of Buber's sense of Hitlahavut, the "ardor of ecstasy . . . all bounds sink before its boundless step. The world is no longer its place: it is the place of the world . . . [It] can appear at all places and at all times. Each hour is its footstool and each deed its throne . . . Repetition, the power which weakens and discolors so much in human life, is powerless before ecstasy, which catches fire again and again from precisely the most regular, most uniform events . . . [Or the ecstatic who] When his father-in-law reproved him for [being found in the streets and gardens and groves] answered with the parable of the hen who hatched out goose eggs, 'And when she saw her children swimming about on the surface of the water, she ran up and down in consternation seeking help for the unfortunate ones; and did not understand that this was their whole life to them: to roam on the surface of the water.' "

And the language finds accord in the words of Lafcadio Hearn to Chamberlain the better part of a century ago: "For me words have color, form, character; they have faces, ports, manners, gesticulations; they have moods, humors, eccentricities;—they have tints, tones, personalities . . . [there were] the whispering of words, the rustling of the procession of letters . . . the pouting of words, the frowning and fuming of words, the weeping, the raging and racketing and rioting of words, the noisomeness of words, the tenderness or hardness, the dryness or juiciness of words,—the interchange of values in the gold, the silver, the brass and the copper of words."

Cowley would have it that for Hearn "Words . . . were the magic spells that protected him from a world of enemies." In Gary's case they also clearly bind him to a world of friends. Words of the tribe. A money. Where whatever profit accrues to whoever wants it, feels it, can use it.

ALL OVER THE DRY GRASSES

>   Motorburn,   oil sump dirt smell
>   brake   drum

—the man's delight in the flatfooted monosyllabic grit noun, words that dig toes, barefoot, in soil. A kind of joy in dirt, the sheer exuberance of contact:

>   clean crumbled creek-washed rotted granite
>   quartz & feldspar   sand.

A satyr with memo, musing:

>   I slept up on your body;
>   walkt your valleys and your hills;

>   sandbox
>   sandpaper
>   sandy.

The child at work, playing. The uninhibited pleasure in words, the verbs less active than the verbal adjectives, the nouns a constant appui:

>   Round smooth stones
>   up here in the weeds
>   the air a grey wet

: words, weights, poises, poses—ways of sitting, ways of shitting, meditating: so much for nothing. And friends

>   Masa bending on the rocks
>   Staring close to the water,
>   Nanao and Nagasawa
>   with their lifted cups of shochu,

>   Friends and poets
>   Eating, drinking in the rain,
>   and these round river stones.

A camaraderie that extends into and through the landscape around above and below.

There can be a surfeit of words, as in the same poem ("By the Tama River at the North End of the Plain in April"—the explicit nature of the man's approach to where he is at):

> Grilling raw squid over smoky twigs
> a round screen perched on broken bricks

where "raw" and "smoky" could be left out at no loss to the imagination. But the scene is his and he makes it acutely so, unmistakably.

In "The Wide Mouth," where haikai begin to be suggested, the Kyoto locus touches into a large nativeland, American Indian talk, after the sparrow "shew/his wide pink   mouth" (the vowel coloring of an old past tense, to give it more tenseness):

> Not a sound,
> white world,
> great trouble.

The throwback to America within the moment of building snowfall.

He likes these connections, continents falling together mainly out of a conjoint experience, one of the most widely travelled poets of our time.

The various breakfast scenes known "In the House of the Rising Sun" ending up with transmitted sicknesses:

> New Asian strains of clap
> whip penic   ill in.

Unable to let the play of the word pass unnoticed: pricked by that high C/ seen.

Into the closing strains of guilt:

> blue as Shiva—
> did I drink some filthy poison
> will I ever learn to love?

> Did I really have to kill my sick, sick cat.

And *no* questionmark to debate the matter, really. The open use of digression building moving always back in to where things are, or

158

out and in, somewhat like friend Whalen.

"White Devils" bringing up atrocities and making the feeling in the face of these stick:

> a disembowelled, half-skinned
> horse-sized white wolf bitch
> lying on its side in a pool of
>   half-melted snow,
> a snowbank around her,
> icy melt water staining red,
> the red of blood spreading into the white snow.
>   she moved, stirred,
>
> And I thought, my God.
> still alive.

Here the explicitness has a certain ambiguity about it, Gary both attracted and revulsed by the scene, unsure of his drift into sensual appreciation, evasion of a sort, until the slight motion shakes him back, awakens him to exclamation, inner, quiet. And the punctuation, precise, stops in its own tracks. and says.

The Songs of the second section are openly sensual, the intermingling of bodies, of all living things, interpenetrations:

> Two thigh hills hold us at the fork
>   round mount center
>
> . . . .
>
>   cicada singing,
>   swirling in the tangle
>
> the tangle of the thigh
>
>   the brush
>   through which we push.

The sexual im-pulse, input, so put out, can seem so enthusiastic as to mute more difficult and authentic relation—but Gary is not Creeley. Here the self revealed, known, the gnothi, is

> seed-prow   [seedproud?]
>
> moves in and makes home in the whole.

The play on "whole" transparent.

Gary = boat man. The explication of body as embodied feeling, the unimagined felt. Here thought is feeling. And in "Song of the View," his cunt poem, the insistence felt is upon the clinging, the being held fast within. Tossed back to breast and womb.

"Song of the Taste," one of those he relishes to read, as at Berkeley this past November to a thousand or more assembled, who ate it up attentively:

> Eating roots grown swoll
> inside the soil

where the "swoll" swells into the next line/word to reach its apex.

> Eating each other's seed
> eating
> ah, each other.

The poems are swellings, expansions, expansive. "Kyoto Born in Spring Song" a simple celebration for the long-awaited arrival of the first born. The delectation and the feeling of having joined the life-circle again burst forth gently:

> Mouse, begin again.

> Bushmen are laughing
> at the coyote-tricking
> that made us think machines

> wild babies
> in the ferns and plums and weeds.

The 3rd section goes back to the island, Suwanose. The cooperative community.

If you read of the Banyan Ashram in *Earth House Hold* the key articles of Gary's ecological faith, or hope, or charity?, are entered openly: ". . . in the relationship established by hunting: like in love or art, you must become one with the other . . . putting [the] mind in an open state . . ."

"No marriage is complete if you don't eat tai afterwards, the noble, calm AUSPICIOUS FISH of Japan . . ."

BURNING ISLAND

O Wave God   who broke through me today
    Sea Bream
    massive pink and silver
    cool swimming down with me watching
          staying away from the spear

The poetry and prose fall together: "The sweet-potato field got cleared and planted . . ."

As we hoe the field
    let sweet potato grow
And as sit us all down when we may
To consider the Dharma
    bring with a flower and a glimmer.
Let us all sleep in peace   together.

Bless Masa and me as we marry
    at new moon   on the crater
This summer.

Or: "It is possible at last for Masa and me to imagine a little of what the ancient—archaic—mind and life of Japan were. And to see what could be restored to the life today. A lot of it is simply in being aware of clouds and wind."

Ceremony and celebration more than cerebration. A hymn and a prayer for new marriage.

Carrying relation, in the "Regarding Wave" section of the book, towards new birth, son Kai. But the spadework and what is entailed:

ROOTS

Draw over and dig
The loose ash soil
Hoe handles are short,
The sun's course long
Fingers deep in the earth search

Roots, pull them out; feel through;
Roots are strong.

Chinese in feel, heft; almost T'ao Ch'ien. Or E. P.

A man alone at his work, touching ground, exactitude. But the work is speech, in fact—for this man is not a farmer, his regard is for the communication, that others know, feel, this.

Much of the urge to concrete nouns, names, mantric utterance, is self-directed, to confirm body as fact, in act, in relation. The cry is implicit.

The great drone
In the throat of the hill
The waves drum
The wind sigh.

Declaration of relation: one cannot be too explicit, not enough of feeling, or to be lost exhausting it:

some of the American brag, the youthfulness pushed, the man nearing 40:

Climb delicately back up the cliff
    without using our hands.
    eat melon and steamed sweet potato
    from this ground.
We hoed and fished—
    grubbing out bamboo runners
    hammering straight blunt
    harpoon heads and spears
        Now,
    sleep on the cliff
    float on the surf
    nap in the bamboo thicket
        eyes closed,
    dazzled ears.

Some of it goes back to the remembrance of work songs, here made more personal and delicate.

Much is photographic, cinematic, documentary, remembrance of things past, to be stored up in this immediate release:

careless and joyous.

162

And Kai's arrival—bringing all readers into family. And yet even as he says in "Not Leaving the House":

> I quit going out
>
> Hang around the kitchen—make cornbread
> Let nobody in.

I recall our first visit to him at that time, here in Kyoto, the message on the door saying that nobody should visit. We had brought cake and a paper carp, the boy's holiday being near. And of course there was, despite, cordiality. The desire to husband the event—letting poetry share:

> making a new world of ourselves
> around this life.
> . . . .
>
> The Voice
> is a wife
> to
>
> him still.

2

The rest of the book, additional poems, falls into two sections, one a mixed bag of occasional pieces, political talk, elegy, etc., and the final one of short pieces, closer to haiku—spurts of brio, snaps.
The idea is "Communionism"

> & POWER
> comes out of the seed-syllable of mantras.

His influence on Ginsberg and that flowing back.
The pop pieces here draw me least, as the utterance tries to assume larger costume, public style. It comes more persuasively as it moves back into sensuous particular:

> Fat buds, green twigs,
> flaky gray bark;

163

Flap up together.

The catch of us being in such simple phrases as "flap up"—where a man's rooted restraint that often exceeds itself in trying to prove itself free naturally disengages and opens through what just comes to mouth, unthought.

> the way the words join
> the weights, the warps,
>
> I know   what it means.
> my language is home.

This is beyond dispute. And the return to, noun noun noun name and the name with more action in it than any verb he comes up with virtually:

> salt;   cold
> water;   smoky fire.
> steam, cereal,
> stone, wood boards.
> bone awl, pelts,
> bamboo pins and spoons.
> unglazed bowl.
> a band around the hair.

Or:

> blueblack berry on a bush turned leaf-purple
>
> deep sour, dark tart, sharp
> in the back of the mouth.

The body of language, language of body. The tongue, mouth, taste, touch, feel feel here.

And it ties in too with manufactured items realized as words:

> steel spring-up prongs on
> the back of the Hermes
> typewriter—paper holders . . .

Or:

> pop-top beer tabs in the gravel.

Random notes: trying to work, be in the language that is there where he is, joins us:

> a murmur in the kitchen
> Kai wakes and cries—

Or:

> the knots of snot in kleenex . . .

> Let me unflinching burn
> Such dross within
> With joy
> I pray!

(A touch of Sengai, the zazen man back to us watching ten years pile of shit burning: smoky fire, smelly fire.)

History, autobiography, wherever he is: "The Way Is Not a Way." Work on land, work at sea, and the momentary pauses that suddenly gape upon earth and water, sky and peak.

> A wind moves
> Like a word

> waves

> The face
> Is a ground
> Land
> Looks round.

Wherever you open the poem delight occurs:

The same first bird chirps at the first light.

> hair, teeth, spit, breath,
> backbone, asshole, hip joints, knees,
> ball of the foot.
> knuckles, back of the hands.
> piss-hard-ons at dawn.
> Lazy to get up and snuff the chilly sand
> crap by lantern light.

The man as male asserting, adventure-sized, his masculinity; a sense of the shock of the frank word put down squarely, faced.

Explicit beyond doubt, and yet by the very explicitness making one doubt. Needing to say I AM I AM I AM—meaning AINT I?

> fuzz—burrs—thorns—tiny hairs stickers,
> fluff—down—stickem. fly or be carried
> be ate and be shat out.

> moving the seed around.

> Two Ravens talk a bit,
> Then fly off
> In opposite directions.

The perfect film clip of little Kai "Meeting the Mountains" at Sawmill Lake. And like friend Philip, Gary often likes to date and locate poems, making the personalness stick.

The mythic pitch, reaching Apollinaire:

> Air, fire, water, and
> Earth is our dancing place now.

The rarer sudden elegiac note, "For Jack Spicer," felt:

> You leave us free to follow:
> banks and windings
> forward:
> and we needn't *want* to die.   but on, and
> through.

> through.

And, as often, the poet shows through in his language capacity, to make words move effectively, setting them right on page and punctuating them so. So that the final "through" has quiet ache in it too.

"Long Hair," the title poem of the section that ends with it, is a "sure fire" piece and no wonder he is inclined to read it in public. It is vintage Snyder: coolly playfully inventive, charming and more tenderly ecological than the polemical verse. No point quoting in full, but that the fulness is wanted. I can still hear the man loving his own words in his quiet deliberate voicing:

> Waist high through manzanita,

166

Through sticky, prickly, crackling
   gold dry summer grass.
Ending high with that extra little whoop:

And deer bound through my hair.

3

The final section, brevities, "Target Practice," tinges with
images, tingles—bits that sound back to *Riprap:*

   pack-string of five mules
      winding through the mountain meadow—
   watching us: not thirty yards away
   a great calm six-point buck
      head up, ears front,
   resting deep in flowers.

Reminds me of such visions from W. H. Hudson.
   Mountains and city claim him for his sensed particulars. Echoes,
edges, subsidences to keep a hold of. Not to let go:

      in the dusk
      between movie halls
      the squeak of the chain
      of swings

Childhood claiming claimed.

      pissing

      watching

      a waterfall

Or: finally:

      When creeks are full
      The poems flow
      When creeks are down
      We heap stones.

There are two quotes I'd add to all these from Gary's offerings—from Buber—articulating beyond any comparison where poetry is livingdying, where we come in if we are ready to go out:

"Only living with the other is justice."

"To feel the universal generation as a sea and oneself as a wave, that is the mystery of humility."

29 April 1971

Through

a consideration of *The Prefiguration*
of Frank Samperi   (Mushinsha/Grossman, 1971)

> Each mortal thing does one thing and the same:
> Deals out that being indoors each one dwells;
> Selves—goes itself; *myself* it speaks and spells,
> Crying *What I do is me: for that I came.*

Samperi is a religious poet. He feels himself bound to the faith of Dante and Aquinas and Bonaventura. I am not, and am not qualified to consider his work in relation to that faith. My response can only be to the poetry that comes through. Comes across.

The Hopkins quoted above deliberately does not continue into the vaster denouement, which is even more relevant, perhaps, to where Samperi is at—yet its absence may sound it more, just as Christ as such is absent in his poetry.

To read Hopkins or Samperi, for me at least, requires no suspension of either disbelief or belief. I hear what they say to the extent that I can and to that extent precisely my own words follow.

A man in the middle way, or an innocent, for he is innocent. His eyes see beyond judgment, though the body's needs brought to society bring him to critique.

The earlier poems are lonelier and even more imaginary, a man talking to himself always, trying to make sense, if only to himself, seeing himself dying, seeing himself dead, his body roped to a raft by vagrants and children, with lilies and seaweed,

                                        the raft
           adrift.

In a sense he comes on like the Noh, from way back, posthumously in the guise of a native of New York, or Brooklyn, but clearly, transparently, a spirit.

These are all poems—of this large collection—composed of 7

169

books—of a contemplative quietness—of a deliberate calmness—carefulness. Like his quietly nervous handwriting, unhurried, in the core of his chosen words.

The routine of every day. The usual and the return, never having left, himself, one self.

One poem after another:

> I shall be in the room
> and I shall be glad.
>
> .   .   .   .   .   .
>
> I am in
> the room again.
>
> . . .
>
> I am lying on
> my back in bed.

Desultory.

> I waste
>
>   my afternoons
>   in streets
>
> where faces
>
>   drift . . .

Exact. Finding occasional connections: Mozart tunes or the words of an old man sounding his unspoken words "Damn it, / there's something / wrong / with this place," waiting for a bus.

The city a package deal.

Here, as throughout the book, the thin lines and the wide margins suggest a man threading his way through the towering city's weight.

The shortest poems often suggest an opening, a love of the page's white space—and Samperi is extremely careful in his layout (and the publisher has followed it precisely).

Movement is backwards, the past, or sorrel horses galloping along a dirt road that is itself moving—to a standstill? Or a train, magician, covering distances, exposing a sudden vision of continuity.

Always in a room, looking out a window, or from a train, or even on the street, eyes peering out of the flesh, the stranger within, trying to compose, discompose or recompose, the scene. The seen.

The vow is, haplessly, poverty. The condition largely accepted, facing a possible, living it, integrity:

> for I have paid
> my debts, and having neither father nor mother nor
> brother nor sister, I am now granted freedom—
> which is the quickest way to death. But I swear I shall
> die happy.

Later, he wonders at earlier work, like this, whether he can abide by it. But the past is what we are or there could be no present.

He will not compete, follow the trends, his audience is with God. The ultimate principle,

> the light that swallows blindness.

In his windowless tower the solitary Prince, Nerval's and reiterated Eliot's.

But openings occur, sun rises and sun sets.

The simple occasions of any place: the way light revolves and touches whatever is near, in sight, birds and people, the sounds, the movement of a funeral, a shore. And still from a vantage point: where am I?

> the window
> looks
>
> and sees.

The same events noted without any rhetorical flourish, content with crumbs: birds scattered by children on a city street:

> one flies
> up
>
> to a
> window ledge.

We know the poet is reached. Where he is at. He defines his plight as his position:

> . . . I have always wanted new sights—
> Such as, the movement of a leaf

171

Struggling to free itself from a branch.
But I also know that if free I shall fall.
So I stay with my books, and sometimes make songs.

It is better, I mean, to be here,
Where the mind can act
And make light where there is none,

Than with the crowd, whose mouth defies the sun.
No I can never go; it is dark beyond my gate;
And my mind could not live out there.

Not that, in fact, he hasnt tried since, but his sense of it early on
is accurate, or accurate enough to his limits.

Along with the impulse to song is an impulse to meditate the
sources and sense of the song, the difficulties of bringing the cry into
melody.

If prescient then knowing
of Its beginnings is with Him,
if beginning can be
applied to It—

since even before the battle
He knew of It:
being that Is—

and since good, therefore, It couldn't *be* from Him:
but maybe, It *is* with Him as His "I Am Not."

The music of such poetry—or the poetry of such music—is of so
tacit an order that it easily passes through the ear without regard, yet
there is remarkable subtlety in the little shifts, the dance within the
syllables, where the meaning moves out:

The Christ of meadows,
lost, prayerfully
awaits
a sunrise.

And the satyrs' lithe

172

```
movements tempt
the candor
of his aliveness.
```

Here the seemingly abstract words take on body and action beautifully. (I see that Christ has one reference in this book after all.)

There are gracenotes that remind me of Zukofsky, a poet must begin somewhere and Samperi, who found Zukofsky on his own, started at a rich source, but has long since moved into his own thing, is himself source now, resource.

Often the images recur—like "the broken / head / of a Cupid." But the images are generally of the most natural provenance: tree and hill and field and sky and sea and bird, etc. Dogs and cats, etc., are rarer than birds, and flowers and snow, the sun and sky, more common than birds.

Much of his intent is felt in his own expression of it:

```
to sing of a rose
against a sunrise
and of a man
moving toward water.
```

Since we have him from the start on a raft, a dead Ulysses, but an unbroken Orpheus, we can constantly feel him moving toward water. The very flow of his words, even when they trickle in his channels, is toward the sea.

The places come sharper and with clearer desolation:

```
How long I've leaned against the screen-door!
Our porch empty of the few guests we've ever had;
And the white roses, under the shadeless window
That looks toward the freight yard—dead, too.
```

Toward: the word keeps coming back. Gently.

Toward Kyoto, after the West Coast, an effort from marriage to move out more, children, and back to the big city, unable to leave it, religiously lost in his own place.

```
The roses, song, droop
        On the trellis;
    Dried petals, shadows
Are this garden's music.
```

At a time when poetry makes a fetish of screaming and pointing at itself, when shock-effects are all the rage, this reflective, soft, but tough poetry may easily be overlooked and only slowly overheard. But heard it will be.

> Come
> scatter
> the garden's
> blossoms
>
> on the hill
> above
> the beach! an old man
>
> under
> an umbrella
> lies toward
> water
>
> where a ship
> sails out
> beyond
> a cliff.

Perhaps what moves most is the tenacity in being so straight, so clear, so true—in the face of "the odds." Or muting them by starting from death and realizing backwards.

The landscapes and cityscapes are spare as the words are, simple, shaped by particular insight, allowed what clarity adheres, to let light.

> Nothing so good
> as this thought
> of green under light
> wherein branch
>
> over branch against
> sun moves toward
> its green under
> a guise of light.

Maskless. Nothing intervening that isnt there and by being there, so regarded, relevant—drawn in drawn on.

The all-encompassing, so that all directions come out right, no matter how perceived and entered. Walks. With or without companions. Moving through landscape.

Birds shifting from tree to roof now at the rumbling El, now a branch "in bloom" "trembles under the / lighting of birds." Light within the distances, memories, shadows, snow. Phœnix birds, fire birds. Birds of the light and of the shade.

> A wind's in the persimmon tree—
> Come under its rustling.

As often Samperi allows the referent pronominal adjective its ambiguity, commingling.

The city making dreams:

> . . . a drunk shivering in a doorway—
> a falling toward dream
> or a wandering
> among trees along
> a river

> . . . [another] dream
> of a cliff
> crumbling away from under him
> . . .
> a man
> walks in a meadow
> casting least
> shade
> —Come sit
> under a tree
> in the shadow of the farthest hill;
> there, before you,
> a river

> and the flamingoes.

The paradisal is given color by the sudden exotic birds. To come through to paradise, the dream still. The journey, the walk on so many levels.

Family (Dolores, wife; Claudia, daughter) gives the songs clearer direction:

> Dolores,
> now I make
> my songs
> for you—
> I don't need
> a window . . .

Back in the routine, the boundaries becoming place:

> . . . go sit in the park
> or maybe
> on the bench
> in front of
> the bus stop
> by the hospital
> at least until
> the sun goes
> down

Perhaps no one has ever set these things so plainly and decisively down. And the very plainness provides weight. There is nothing to persuade us of.

The section/long poem "Morning and Evening" is the most ambitious undertaking in the book; it leads to the penultimate "Crystals"—which uses a similar discursive movement toward poetry, but is considerably briefer.

He states his "theme" at the very start and slowly explains precisely what it means, where he's at, what he's doing—so that all critique becomes superfluous.

> A man going away to sorrow . . . dying.

Morning/evening wandering his city. The image involved he explains:

> The morning and evening knowledge of the angels is
> a refinement of the principle of individuation: that is,
> to know things in God and things in themselves is to
> know angelically. . . .

When it is said that the angels behold God's wisdom,
the meaning is: dwelling in His City . . .

So: "To gather a spirit up out of its own conscious." To walk around
the city, his own place, where he is, with his own kind, and find out
the poetry of it, in it.

The extensive prose commentary, which has the economy of
poetry and leads into the sequence of songs at the end (or the
beginning/the opening?), is contemplative in character. A man
communing with his burgeoning spirit:

Concerning an angel dying by a river and a man
sorrowing in a street and the nature of the prefiguration of the one of the other depending upon whether
one's by a river or in a street . . .

Samperi brings most of the preceding poetry back into the
"argument" here as visionary substance. And discusses, inwardly,
letting us join him, the sense of what he is up to:

If a work is primarily addressed to God (thought of as
a "conceptual limit"), then it follows that the audience isn't essential . . .

Essential or not, he persists for us. It is hard to imagine God needing
him.

But the elevation and/or scope sought, moved toward, is
enough. "Conversations with oneself . . . if you walk a street and
come out with a presupposition that is a plain whose perspective is
homeric, then you are as they say in the world but not of it."

The transfiguration forthcoming, we are given presentiment of,
not only in Dante, here, is toward the flow, of song.

He discusses with himself some of the various problems of the
poet and himself as poet in the contemporaneous.

Merit "doesn't work here."

. . . no reason to write seems to be the honest action,
that is, of course, if we accept audience as end, but
since God is the reason we write, then it follows that
the perspective that is historical is pointless.

Samperi's thrust is toward the eternal, the timeless, of it, in it.
What Margaret Mead calls the "postfigurative." The "prefigurative,"

in her cultural reduction, refers to the situation we have now found ourselves in in America and Europe where the young are more reciprocally educating their elders. But this isnt Samperi's prefiguration. He is in the tracks of the angelic.

He realizes how "work in progress" has become touchstone for our time, in passing.

> One wishes to write honestly: therefore, is it honesty to be concerned primarily with the rhythm of language? isn't the triumph in the very vanquishing of language? . . . Logic is circular: is the angelic nature circular?

He is sharp with himself:

> such words! they place me in direct relation to my daily walks—people move I move—rapidly: is the street the river? the sidewalks its banks? buildings a wood's tallest trees? is a man insane to see distortion of this sort? or is it really the builder who in the withdrawal from "the natural whose presupposition is creation" impedes the will only to make it take stock, that is, unlearn the learning, come finally to the glory that laid no traps?

The powers of man and angelic powers. "Let there be words" he says in a passage that knows itself

> to express a child's gaze at moon: in father's arms, she points at the moon and says: bird! not knowing the moon's name—then hearing its name, she delights in it—says it over and over—they pass the shops, the avenue busy as ever; and then at a corner father sees the moon just a little to the side of an apartment building—he reminds; child says again over and over: moon moon . . . : sleep my child heavenly under moon!
>
> What constitutes a true definition of sentimentalism? a risk involving a man in a past whose ambience is sensible? should an angel look down upon a man? God forbid!

The problem of work, or the answer of work? It doesnt work, or what he is doing is his work. "There's movement in air but it isn't light."

Depression. "There can be no audience when a work's vision is total." But Samperi's vision doesnt preclude his seeing the errors of a city:

> . . . why parks built within city rather than cities built within park. . . To a man whose shoes are falling apart a movement toward a park is a movement toward unearthly existence.

Or where poverty leads *him*. The heavenly gutter?
The victims or spirits of poverty reviewed.
The city, the city, bringing him to his work:

> To write as if every substantive were not valid unless first adjectivally qualified—this presupposition's behind even the most austere work . . .

> If there's longing for confraternity with the angels, then every movement a man makes to establish such is a movement toward specific difference.

> Following again the way downward, you come to an impasse that shows you to yourself as the maker of your own obstacles—but once clear of the impasse, which presupposes that the way out is thru the realization that accuses oneself, an image of deeper clarity comes thru: you as victim.

> To use *you* is to imply *I*.

> Words gathering around a word.

> Beloved's the word that gathers . . .

> Sing the stars the angels the angels the stars.

> Poverty seems to be the only action capable of reducing an intensity of activity.

The poetry, succinct, follows:

the

angel

passed

thru

the

city

and

moved

up

and

down

trusting

in

the

path

. . . Then over to the waterfront
ships
and beyond
hills
and everywhere
falling
snow

"Crystals" picks up the theme of poverty, spirit, contemplation as work, as against all exploitation:

It all amounts to this: if a man is capable of knowing completely, then his companions are the angels.   To say that a man's knowledge is face to face is to say that the vision is never at odds with the life.

A man's proper prefiguration is his proper stance.

. . . nothing that one man or another can say can place the meaning unequivocally there rather than here. What is intended is a boundary that reduces each man's movement to a movement essential in the sense that the ambience is but a projection of his inner state.

Reading Samperi's arguments is not a study in logic; this is poetry, whatever the form it seems to assume. His prefiguration, if you will. Where he takes himself is where he is at. Unless one is to take his place, subsume it, which is quite impossible, one cannot *judge* the argument. Only move with it, feel something of his journey from and through the depths, as it attains a reasonable clarity, as it reaches towards the sea:

> the wood's clearer
> because of the children
> gathering flowers
> along its paths

*

"So Close"—brief love poems—closes the collection: body touching body:

> Body to body our night less boundary than fragrance
> releases bird hill river

*

The stone prints by friend Will Petersen palimpsest the opaque surface with the resistances of color, defining edges, self-defined, finding event written unreadably upon rock. No name and no dates.
What follows will be more beginning.
Such quiet intensity listens to heart. Hears.

21 May 1971

Appendix

This note from Samperi just received (5/25/71) may be useful to a reader who wants a sense of the poet's intent:

> I must confess that I was overwhelmed by the book. E's (the publisher's) fine sense of structure establishes the *proportions* of the book beyond a doubt—*the malleability of the prose* in harmony with the *longest* poems (the factors determining the ultimate size of the format), plus the ease of the last 6 poems surprisingly resolving the totality of vertical direction. Purity is an element throughout, and that does me a world of good.
>
> ([marginal:] I mean, the whole book seems to be drawn to the top of the page—so in a truly profound sense *So Close* is the finest *aspect* of the vertical.)
>
> It has been my contention that my first 7 books all along look toward each other resolving each other—in fact, it has been my contention that that is my method of composition—and this publication makes that very clear . . .

Add this additional note (6/2/71):

> . . . The *richness* of *The Prefiguration* is implicit—proper names are kept at a minimum: e.g., Augustine is a figure, altho never mentioned by name; even so, simplicity is pursued as a desired end and complexity is rejected as confusion; therefore, the book is in opposition to the modern spirit, but is not out to eradicate it.

With Lorine

a memorial: 1903-1970

My wife and I—on a visit to Fort Atkinson I had promised us for many years—met Lorine and Al on November 15, 1970 (that is, within a few weeks of the stroke that was to claim her life, not poetry, the last day of the year). They had suggested we stay at the Black Hawk Hotel, dowdy, but clean, convenient and reasonable, in the center of the town. It was one day, about 8 hours in all we spent together. We had waited for it.

Inasmuch as few ever met her or had much talk with her (Louis Zukofsky was her mentor and friend almost from the start and it is with him most words were exchanged), let me offer characteristic passages from her letters to me over a period of some ten years; they tell her better than any description can.

She had in October 1964—to celebrate her marriage, her home-making?—made me a handwritten handbound copy of her most recent poems and added a watercolor drawing of the place. Nextdoor to where we found them living when we visited them, near where she was born: Black Hawk Island (Wisconsin). Her little drawing with a pencil frame and sketched in pencil under the light wash depicts a shack with two windows and a door facing near the river (Rock River) that empties just beyond into Lake Koshkonong. Colorful flowers dot the edge of the paths to and by the water. And moored to a small landing a tiny red boat. She wrote:

> I somehow feel impelled to send you the product of
> the last year, just to keep in touch. I know you're not
> printing [*Origin*]. I even brave school kid's paints to
> show you where we live! It's been—*a year!* I wish you
> and Louie and Celia and I could sit around a table.
> Otherwise, poetry has to do it . . .

My first letter from her is dated Sept. 6, 1960:

> Louie explained to me that you probably want to
> print young poets, at least in this issue of *Origin* just
> coming up. But he said I might try anyhow with the
> two most recent poems "Why do I press it: are you
> my friend?" and "In Leonardo's light." Having typed
> those, I show a further lack of the wisdom that should
> go with my years by sending a few others. The short
> poems with Roman numerals have no real sequence in
> case you want to break them up.
>
> Please feel no embarrassment in returning them if
> you have to . . .

If it needs saying, these poems were all accepted and published in the
2nd series of *Origin* and she never sent me work that I wasnt grateful
to print.

On Sept 19, 1960 the next one:

> . . . It gives me pleasure to appear with or "against"
> the young.
> I am enclosing five not yet printed . . .
> I wondered if you would be interested in knowing
> which ones of all the poems I've written I consider my
> best. These are the five I also enclose . . .

The poems she liked best were: "Old man who seined," "Paul / when
the leaves / fall," "I rose from marsh mud," "There's a better shine,"
"The clothesline post is set."

Her judgment I'd not contradict, but would find place for others
as well, early and late. Give me time and I'll quote.

Nov 7, 1960:

> Use the additional 5 in my last letter—I'm so happy
> you like them. My past work sometimes seems a little
> odd to me! . . . if a bit of my pay check at some time
> in the near future will help you, please let me know. I
> eat fairly well. I want to know that you do!

At the beginning of January she saw a note about a new book of
mine and sent me money for a copy—which I never allowed again; she

remarked: "hardly enough to make you believe in Santa Claus."

I had turned a Scottish friend onto her, having had pleasure in his work myself. ". . . I thank whatever gods there be that someone's good hand (could it have been yours?) sent me these poems. Nothing in a long while has reached my particular kind of home like they have. Certainly one third of them have simply set me free . . ." (The book was the Migrant Press edition of Ian Hamilton Finlay's *The Dancers Inherit the Party*.)

Finlay eventually found her work in turn and published a small attractive selection in Edinburgh: *My Friend Tree*.

Jan 23, 1961:

> . . . I wish I weren't so obsessed in my writing with form, a set form, sometimes it helps and then again it hinders . . . I'm enclosing a revision of the poem I sent you: "Why do I press it": Louie likes this new version better and I know that there were dead spots in the first one . . . Ian Hamilton Finlay. This is the first time I've written a fellow poet on my own initiative since that long ago time when I first wrote Louie Zukofsky.

She had seen the Zukofsky Objectivist issue of *Poetry* (Chicago) when it first appeared in February 1931 and it took her six months, she told me, to get up enough nerve to write him. It was effectively the beginning of her career.

July 30, 1961: *"Origin 2*—I'm so proud to be in it . . ."

Feb. 18, 1962:

> . . . That lovely little book *[For Instance]* . . . You now inhabit a corner of my immortal cupboard with LZ (especially the short poems), Emily Dickinson, Thoreau, Lucretius, Marcus Aurelius, John Muir, bits from Santayana, D. H. Lawrence, Dahlberg, William Carlos Williams, and haiku . . . You and Jonathan Williams have thrown off the shackles of the sentence and the wide melody. For me the sentence lies in wait—all those prepositions and con-nectives—like an early spring flood. A good thing my follow-up feeling has always been condense, con-dense . . .

May 8, 1962:

Another flood come and gone. This time not in my house. Muskrats grinding their catch just outside my door in the middle of the night—a heavy door with cracks. Now it's the greenest grass possible, yellow warblers and the smell of honeysuckle bushes and as Ian might say: I canna leave my home . . .

How do you really like them cool Cats [Catullus versions] of Louie's and Celia's? Ah, those in *Origin* 5! Thank you, thank you.

Jan. 3, 1963:

. . . I like to inject some wit but it can become a disease. Sharp wit, I mean . . .
PS The poetry of Robert Kelly interests me very much. Let's watch him.

Jan. 13, 1963:

. . . Passion in sound, noise (the latin of Catullus) (folk); however, isn't it closer to art when it's still enough (deep enough) to become ice? But of course origins let go the drive without which we could do nothing. I'm a little worried—not really, tho—about my own folk impulse lost—lost?—on the way to the ice . . .

Oct. 2, '63:

I expect in a couple of months to retire and live in Milwaukee with my husband . . . Close by the apartment is Lake Michigan with big foreign boats. Next summer my beloved Black Hawk Island again . . .

Earlier: May 13 '63:

. . . *No* flood this spring, very unnatural.
Unnatural, also, my immanent (sic) marriage. At sixty one does foolish things. I hope I'm happy! He's my connection with life.
Till life settles down, this frog is singing silently . . .

186

March 12, 1964:

> Winter almost gone—the winter of my content, married winter among the dark, leaning buildings of old Milwaukee—churches and taverns. Spires, turrets, point-top towers that form on the way up the rounded corners of ornate houses and business places. These copies of Old World spire-effects—in the old days in the Dakotas and probably here, lanterns were hung in the high windows directly under the cone-shaped roofs to light travelers thru storms. This upward—and often ugly—thrust of people everywhere . . .
>
> I'm enthralled, of course, by the big boats here—Lake Michigan, you know. Those huge red ore boats with that terribly *white* superstructure. Lovely parks named for Polish-American Revolutionary patriots. I walk everywhere . . .
>
> . . . retiring at 60 with ten "good" years ahead of me, I should make a fair start at getting to the bottom of it . . .

June 5 '64:

> . . . you're going into a conversational-metaphysical?? (You won't like that word metaphysical any more than I do) but you know what I mean—and going into it faster than I am. All our lives we steer away from it but when we do attain it we know there's nothing like it . . .

Postmarked 12 Dec 1964:

> . . . When I was 18 I bought a Wordsworth and took the book with me down here (mouth of the Rock River) toward evening. I didn't quite know, yet I think I was vaguely aware that the poetry current (1921) was beginning to change . . . I thought this morning as I "painted": painting (and you paint what you love) takes away desire of possessing things. (By the way, if you've ever painted, wasn't it odd the first few times to get the *silence* in that art after being used always to words? You are the only one who can carry over the silence into poems) . . .

Postmarked 8 June 1965:

> . . . we are the long range people . . .

June 17, 1965:

> . . . As you know, I'd be happy if a book of my own poems could come out by some publisher somewhere before I die . . .
>
> Wallace Stevens—I must re-read for "song"—I had the impression that's *all* some of them were!! . . .

July 2 '65:

> . . . there's more to *say* than to write if we could do it that way . . .
>
> . . . I get for the first time that meaning has something to do with song—one hesitates a bit longer with some words in some lines for the thought or the vision—but I'd say mostly, of course, cadence, measure make song. And a kind of shine (or sombre tone) that is of the same intensity throughout the poem. And the thing moves. But as in all poems everywhere, depth of emotion condensed, I'd say. I'd say—rather than write these days . . .

Dec. 3, 1965 (written earlier):

> . . . Now I've sent him the "review" on you and he answers [Morgan Gibson of *Arts in Society*] "The Cid Corman piece is perfect" . . . By the way the U. in Milwaukee asked me to give a poetry reading there but I fight shy of that kind of thing.
>
> Not perfect, the piece, as he said, but I tried—and it's somewhat so . . .
>
> . . . fortifying ourselves on a small turkey in the oven. Routabaga Al must have, sweet potatoes I like, and you can guess cabbage salad. How lovely if you could drop in for dinner. I've brought my bottle of milk of magnesia . . .

Dec. 16, 1965:

188

. . . A book larger than our apartment in Milwaukee and addressed to Sweet Lady Lorine came from Stella Leonardos (Brazilian poet and translator). All I have to do now is find a translator. And add a room to the house.

Feb. 9, 1965:

    . . . somehow we must meet . . .

June 15, 1966:

The issue received—mother and child doing fine I almost want to say!—and a kind fate in Japan saw to it. At first I worried a good deal—letters you said were included [*Origin* 2, 3rd series]—Lordy, what had I said?? But turns out OK. Got the mail in yesterday along with some groceries. I read *Origin* standing up, every line, before putting the meat and milk in the refrigerator. I sweetened while the milk soured . . .

Al is out of work this week because he bumped his leg in the bathtub—these modern conveniences! In my former tiny house I lived several years—12—without plumbing—while my tenants in the two places my father left me had complete bathrooms!

Basil Bunting—yes, I came close to meeting him when he was in this country in the 30's. Some mention at the time of his going into the fishing business (he had yeoman muscles LZ said and arrived in NY with a sextant) with my father on our lake and river but it was the depression . . . I've always enjoyed his poetry . . .

July 16, 1966:

    . . . Strange—we are always inhabiting more than one realm of existence—but they all fit in, if the art is right.

Aug. 20, '66:

Yes, the Lake Superior trip was a great delight if I can make the poem. Traverse des Millens! A millenium of

189

notes for my *magma* opus! . . . [LN's husband's name Millen.]

Second letter of same date:

> . . . I saw the LZ movie! Quite by surprise—was darning socks and looked up and there was LZ walking along with cap and overcoat on—that lope-dance-walk, you know. Oh, older, white hair—longer in the face maybe but *there,* the same as when I saw him last in '54 . . . the talking between readings was lovely and he does it so easily and naturally and with that soft hint of sighing humor . . . The long, skeleton-supple hand reaching for a book or pointing to a couch cover (afghan, I guess) beside him and his saying "I don't think my poetry is any better than this.". . .

Oct. 13, 1966:

> . . . moves me, but why must the show of vitality come by way of misery, dirt, sexiness. No better poetry than the quiet . . .
>
> I can't enter into social meetings . . . since I housekeep—plural: houses—and write and read and walk and sew and sing at the top of my voice when folky records are being played on the phonograph . . .
>
> Pound . . . interview . . . says he's made mistakes, hurts, in fact, everything he touches . . . *If* this is all true, the interviewer truthful as well as Pound, and if P. actually is saying: I made a mistake in believing in fascism, in being a poet with a cruel edge, arrogant feelings etc. . . . *that* combined with his old age nobility now—one could almost faint over it. It stops me as tho I were in the landscape of one of your poems. What do you think . . . ?

[On the outside:]

Funny, I can't get the roaring, ranting, filthy, spiritual *Kaddish* out of my mind.

190

Dec. 15, 1966:

. . . Am I the American indeed—I can't be entirely content, it seems, without some puzzlement, some sharpness, a bit of word-play, a kind of rhythm and music in however small a way . . .

. . . does one need a poet's life to get at his poetry? Perhaps so, never struck me so, really.

March 2, 1967: (at U of Wis–Milw):

. . . JW read . . . But gave me a large mention there and a few people came up to me to shake hands. I couldn't help as I looked around at that quiet little gathering of somewhat select persons what it would be like to live in a community of poets! a little too cold to speculate while there and by now each one of us is an isolate dot on the page again . . .

March 15, 1967:

Snowing. Well here they are—I never let a poem out without *some* trepidation tho all the alternatives seem to have been whirled thru the air and shoveled away . . .

May 3, 1967:

. . . These movies today—the pavement is wet in the picture and you move your feet in the theatre for fear they'll get wet too . . .

I've thought so much about poems read aloud and poems printed—with me a tendency to greater drama if spoken (aware of not simply audience but mixed and nerve-crossed audience, of somewhat inattentive audience), to more words, to prose but of a heightened kind. So compromise, but then you lose a tight, perfect kind of poetry. Also why compromise printed poetry with musical composition i.e. notations of pause, chant, loud . . . you'd want some scenery also and then you'd have stage drama or movie. Poems are for one person to another, spoken thus, or read silently. How would the bug on the branch, walking to the end of it, or the raindrop there—your poems—be read to a hall filled with people? If I close my eyes I look for the words on the page . . .

You speak of Celia's music in connection with Noh—quite plausible. I've never seen a Noh play but somehow have an idea of it . . . her music . . . I know I'd never heard music so strange but so absolutely quietly impressive . . . till Celia played *Pericles* on the piano and Louie spoke-sang it.

I'd like not to be steeped in traditional music—O to be as free from that as I am from traditional church religion.

May 18 '67:

Well, now, you will be coming to USA! and to Milwaukee if possible . . . I do want to talk with you . . .

July 12, 1967:

Basil came! . . . I took them to a tea room in Fort for lunch. Basil: "I don't suppose it would be possible to get a glass of beer here?" Have you ever met him?—his manner is timid and tender. Withal so kindly. O lovely day for me . . . And of course the question came up of reading poems aloud. The world is mad, MAD on this subject. Would somebody would start Meditation Rooms, places of silence, so silent you couldn't help but hear the sound of your page without opening your mouth and reading books would come back . . .

Oct. 13, 1967:

. . . and yesterday my going to see *Ulysses* . . . I was more concerned with the extremely long and steep escalator up and down (theatre is upstairs)—the boy who took the ticket stopped the crazy thing for me so I could get on and at the top I stepped very high. I must study it sometime, a question of eyes rather than motion . . .

. . . Louie . . . writes me that the group of mine in *Origin* 7 is "mostly my very best"—Wild, wild praise . . .

Cid—feel perfectly free to not print me—tho saying that I feel lost . . .

Oct. 24, 1967:

. . . Probably all it means is another long stretch of geologic time before anything really gets printed. The only time the lava flows is those moments while the poems are being written. I should remind them tho, that they don't see time as I do who haven't too much more of it . . .

Nov. 8 '67:

Coming out of a severe illness—a wrenched back apparently from working outdoors. I sawed down two small trees etc. They say woman's place is in the home, begin to believe it . . .

Dec. 7, 1967:

. . . "Wintergreen Ridge" . . . suits *Origin* so much better and really is I think the best thing I've ever done . . .

. . . I was not made to go to Sunday school or church sessions as a child and I can say now like Henry James and William who didn't go either: I didn't have so much to unlearn when I grew up. I wouldn't discard the Bible, tho, by any means. The other day a friend . . . lent me a book by a Swedenborgian minister . . . it sent me flying to Plotinus Plato and—Swedenborg! And after that to all my natural science reading. Geology has done so much for me! . . .

. . . NY paper the other day shows Marianne Moore with a haunted look (still wears no glasses) in her eyes, a wonderful eighty-year-old look, wondering, no doubt, why the library she was visiting should be built with a feudal look . . .

193

Dec. 29, 1967:

. . . the poem I had hoped would come forth by Christmas is not to be—it's wintering in a grub stage, only hope it transmutes into something as nice looking as the dragonfly next summer—the kind of thing I mean is in the air, Cid, it will be done by somebody else if I don't—then again maybe I'm all wrong or I can't do it: would have to be painted or put into music notation . . .

Jan. 10, 1968:

Well, that brown book in a brown slip-case—the feel and look and even smell of tree and ground and sedge. I wrote Eshleman immediately: Cid has crossed the Barrier. I remembered much of it from an *Origin* of a few years back. Here—I think this is it—the ultimate in poetry. The hard and clear with the mystery of poetry—and it's done largely by the words omitted. Stark, isolated words which must somehow connect with each other and into the next line and the sense out of the sound. (Of course Basho himself must have been very complex) . . .

. . . my reading list . . . But all this won't be remembered, likely, when I open the door out home beside the marsh some spring night and hear the sora rail running down the scale—the spoon-tapped water glass . . .

Feb. 14, 1968:

. . . Been carrying on a correspondence with Eshleman. Mostly at his behest—technique, why I don't write differently, why he doesn't. I'm no good at it—I write from notes, which seem to always stay notes, grocery lists. I throw up my arms and scream: Write—cut it and just write poems. I tell him why set fire to page after page, why not arrest it at moments into quiet, enduring love? (I *dared* to say this.) Also that there is such a thing as silence—and the great, everpresent possibility that our poems may not get read. Art is cooler than he thinks.

Remember Duncan saying quite a few years ago: "I like rigor and even clarity as a quality of a work . . . as I like muddle and floaty vagaries . . . cloudy art . . . It is the intensity that moves me." Well, I told Clayton that many times I like his short poems. I get caught up in merely a fiery nebula when it comes to *Walks*. Good for me at this time since as you've surmised, I've been going thru a bad time—in one moment (winter) I'd have thrown over all my (if one can) years of clean-cut, concise short poem manner for "something else" (still don't know what to call it). I think *Walks* helps me to go straight, however! A glimpse at the work of Koch and Ashbery and I'm quite sure I've been doing OK for a long time.

If we could talk . . .

March 7, 1968:

. . .Clayton thought I needed loosening and finally advised I take 25 micrograms of LSD! Four letters on each side passed between us, he wanted to print 'em, I said NO . . . I've made a turnabout again toward the short poem, don't feel I shd. leave what's been a part of me all these years . . . I can't vouch for Al staying interested in my literary work to the extent of selling it after I'm gone . . .

May 21, 1968:

. . . Lovely day in Madison. I found Louie not de-pressed . . . not so much that as weary from his previous day. I find letters don't do it (over a period of 14 years, no! since I saw him and Celia)—talking clears the air and brings out half a laugh here and there. A glance and a certain tone makes all the difference. We poor beings with what we think—life is made up of more and what strikes the feelings directly *that's* our best way—one person facing another . . .

June 12, 1968:

. . . We feel happy you'd like to see us, Cid . . .

195

August 1st '68:

> . . . I don't suppose there's ever been much going away adventure in my blood except those half dozen times (less than that, I think) I went to NYC many years ago. I'll wait for you to come this way and then we'll surely talk . . .

Oct. 4, 1968:

> . . . Reason we want to leave Black Hawk Island the place of my birth and where I have a grave with my name on it is . . . pollution . . . a wrench, of course, to separate myself even if only in thought, from my *home* to take up another where and what . . .

Dec. 27 '68:

> . . . Doloroso and yesterday on way to doctor I wondered if it were not death. No, not quite that bad but he mentioned an erratic heart beat and now I have digitalis and a row of tone-building and gas-moving medicines . . . etc . . . I don't feel it's serious tho I do feel slowed up considerably these days . . .

(When we finally met, her body was visibly feeble; she trembled almost continuously and was evidently doing more work around the house than was wise.)
Feb. 4, 1969:

> Can't remember when I last wrote you—I've been in the hospital for x-rays, tests etc . . . I fainted one midnight there and had to have 7 or 8 stitches taken to the back of the head . . . I guess I can no longer run a race with a child. (You probably know, I'm 65.) But a few strokes with the hoe among the tulips this spring—that I do count on . . .
>
> February so far has been cold but nice here ((still in Milwaukee))—very little snow and ice just now. I walk a mile to post office and walk back . . .

Feb. 21 '69:

> I forgot—the most important thing—your planned visit to the US in 1970—will be retired then . . .

May 7, 1969:

A long time since I last wrote—I live very happily until I'm 65 then a young musician writes some poetry in *Origin* 13 and I'm in anguish! But I've backed down quite a bit on abstractionism in poetry—as LZ suggests: what is empty is empty, and who wants it? He has chosen the very three poems of Daive I had considered the height of poetry. I'm content to let these stand—p 20, 56, 58. You get to wondering if most of those Daive pages are subverted not by emptiness either but maybe by thought!

I'm absorbed in writing poems—sequence—on William Morris. I know how to evaluate—Ruskin etc., their kind of socialism—paternalism—but the letters of Morris have thrown me. Title will be *His Carpets Flowered*. I can't read his poems. I'd probably weary of all those flowery designs in carpets, wall papers, chintzes . . . but as a man, as a poet speaking to his daughters and his wife—o lovely.

Speaking of lovely—the Kusano book and there is that frog again. You get the idea here is a fine person and very human. Consider Kusano in contrast to Daive—humanity, I mean. I wish you could thank him for me for the book . . .

Lovely to talk on the phone with LZ a couple of minutes Monday—he and Celia going to London May 12 for two weeks or three—he reads at the Camden Festival and at US Embassy—all expenses paid—it gives them a kind of vacation, I'm so happy . . .

I have a note here: To Cid—the lines of natural growth, of life, unconsciously absorbed from foliage and flowers while growing up. I've lost what it's related to, probably Morris. I'm only glad to be taking the next breath, nowadays . . .

May 28, 1969:

. . . . Out home the beautiful barn swallows darting from river to house, lettuce up, red tulips spindly in the wind, fuzzy white things from willows floating about, grass grass grass to mow into eternity . . .

June 10, 1969:

> . . . To the English, Wisconsin places are all lumped together—the Lake Superior country (to me high, hard, rough, rocks etc . . . is another world from the lowland, the soft, willowy, blackbird singy! of ours on the Rock River—by the way, there—our permanent home after Sept.—we're 60 miles from Milwaukee—only 30 or 35 from Madison . . .

Aug. 28, 1969:

> . . . Packing in, i.e. into house out home, the few pieces of furniture—no room of my own but I have the bedroom pretty much any time of the day with small table and comfortable chair. North window there with a lot of sky—river is on opposite side of house. Small color TV ((it had been replaced with a big one when we arrived)) for UHF (educational network)—I can see color better than black and white altho quite often you see a green face because there's green in the background, likewise beefsteak red and tornado purple . . . My thoughts are with you both even when I don't write letters . . .

Oct. 22, 1969:

> . . . as LZ said long ago: put down what seems valid and strong in your mind and don't destroy it much as you'd like to afterward tho it doesn't sometime later look as good to you as it did at first . . .
>
> Al is reading a story about tulips that think . . . His science has to be fictionalized.
>
> Do get out into the fall—blustery here, tho—good caterpillar hunting.

Dec. 7, 1969:

> . . . Your *Origin* 16—Daphne Marlatt—impressive but to me nothing new matters after the Daive. Montage, yes, it suggests the reality that may get inside us and fill the subconscious of the future! "Several referential planes at any one moment." Is life really so full of broken furniture for her? Are there no

moments when she can arrange the furniture? To put it down as a sensuous harmony?? . . .

I sent University of Wisconsin Milwaukee a copy of *T&G* back in Sept. A few days ago I wrote: Did you fail to receive it? They answer they've placed it with regional materials. I should ask: What region— London, Wisconsin, New York? . . .

Postmarked Jan 8, 1970:

O cold here, ten below last night, 15 the night before. A huge rabbit came to the foot of the bird feeder pole last night for bread. Probably the same one that takes shelter under the overturned boat. A cardinal (we have no church but his) atop the feeder early this morning. It was mass for us. I smile—last 2 sentences somehow accidentally Emily Dickinson! Ugh!—which brings me to the Indian chief who said as he was dying: "No more forever." Which reminds me of the little *no more* received almost a month ago. Ah again so very nice, Cid, and I hope not no more tho it's no more forever . . .

I write from 5:00 to 11:00 mornings—a hard pull with a husband in a small house with me. He reads but likes to mention things he reads sometimes. Just a few minutes ago he spoke of raising corn next spring and saving some of it—on the cob—to shell it later or just let the birds get the kernels off, themselves— "even if they get bits of cob with the corn!" I: Have you ever tasted corncob? He: Yes, it's quite sweet. Another time the subject turns to Charles Russell the painter of Indian and cowboy pictures. He: We kids used to go to the depot to see the calendar—one had Charles Russell's pictures on it. This was in northern Minnesota . . .

Jan. 9 ('70):

Didn't know yesterday when I sent you a letter I'd feel like getting up at 4:30 this morning to finish the *Jefferson* and type it. My hope is to get it into the same issue with the Wm. Morris etc . . .

Feb. 14, 1970:

> Number 17! Here I am in a whirl again—to me Jaccottet as wonderful as Daive, more so. . . . I wish I knew what LZ thought of all this . . . you speak of receiving his remarks—I don't want to trouble you but could you briefly relay them . . . ? . . .

March 7, 1970:

> . . . Rezy, yes, and he must be old now, was I'd say in his 50's when I knew him—gentlest soul possible, afraid he might intrude, afraid to leave his umbrella out in the public hallway and afraid to bring it dripping into the room. For a few years after my New York stay he sent me his books as they came out. What lovely poetry—"sincerity" as Z characterized it in that Feb. '31 *Poetry* Mag . . .
>
> I look out and see winter goldfinches (wild canaries). Strange to see greenish yellow in winter. Red wing blackbirds here storming the trees, a noise-storm, and for three days geese going over with *their* glorious noise. It must mean early spring. No flood expected. Wish you were coming over this spring . . .

March 17, 1970:

> . . . How terrible I've had an undercurrent of hurry this winter—never before a part of my life . . .

May 4, 1970 (misdated 1969):

> Lovely May morning—all green here now, a light warm rain last night, a bit of it still in the tulip cups.
>
> I'm so afraid people won't know about the one rather big review I've had so far (*T&G*)—*The Nation* April 13. By Michael Heller, teacher at New York Univ. He has a nice feeling for the poems. Sometimes a review doesn't mean more than that but without that one wouldn't want a review . . . Carl Rakosi here one day—I'll tell you all about it in November . . .

May 12:

> I'm 67 yrs old today! . . . Emerson—yes! I cd be-
> come deeply interested in that man . . .

June 17, 1970:

> . . . Only thing I mourn is that Tom Jefferson didn't
> get to Diderot in time before his (D's) death. TJ was
> crossing the Atlantic to become Minister to
> France . . .

Aug. 18, 1970:

> . . . I'd better speak of Nov. 18-20 now—I'd like to
> have you and Shizumi for a meal . . . The important
> thing is that you and I have time for talk
> . . . Surely the high moment of my life next to
> having met Louie in New York in 1934 . . .

Aug. 24, 1970:

> . . . I always feel kind of faded out—my way of
> writing—compared to some parts of the *Cantos*. I'm
> the piece of wash that has hung too long in the sun! I
> thought something like this when I first read your
> letter with this news: I'm a little bunch of marshland
> violets offered to the crooked lawyer—O no . . . how
> could I refer to Pound in that way???—I owe so much
> to him as most present-day poets do—and so much of
> the *Cantos* and the other poems of his is so beauti-
> ful . . .
> *Darwin* now finished—good but not as deft as the
> *Jefferson* . . .
> Take care so we see you for sure . . .

Sept. 5, 1970:

> That *Origin* 20! Every poem and the Olson letter. O
> Hitomaro—there he is way back there in the 7th
> century ahead of me! . . .
> If he looked toward the 20th century for his poems
> to reappear it must have been like seeing the stars
> which I suppose he felt would always be there . . .

Her last sentence alludes, as some readers will know, to LZ's *Essay on Poetry*.

She signed off:

> . . . So—with more good wishes for your trip over
> I yam
>   as ever
>   and the one baking squash
>   for dinner—
>   Lorine.

I cannot recall now, but there was surely a postcard or two prior to our visit, since the dates were particularized and I spoke to her from a Fort Atkinson outskirts telephone box, receiving directions to the Black Hawk Hotel. It was about 11 PM, but she and Al retired at sundown always and she thought it was about 2-3 AM.

Perhaps some of my journal notes of the visit might fall properly here, and then a brief sampling of her poems. My words are candid:

15th Nov (Sunday):

> Up about 8:30. Day partly cloudy/cool & bright . . .
> Breakfast (at hotel) about 11 and as figured Al & Lorine came in while we were amidst it. OK. Al a Minnesota backwoodsman: a guy—with a satisfaction in the *manly* formula—gentle at heart, but clumsy. Lorine shy & gentle. Bright & true. Incapable of crudity. Lonely/eager for intellectual company but unable to foment it, fearful of the "larger" scene. Not quite as *bold* as Emily—but a genuine voice & spirit.
>
> Her preparations didn't altogether come off—but *they* were *not* our "reason" for visiting. Al likes his football games, etc. He likes the adventurous & vigorous: the quiet & meditative puts him at a disadvantage & doesnt stir him. He's a fair storyteller & has good stories from childhood to tell. He lacks—however—"realization"—so that the stories can only have whatever depth someone else might draw from them . . .
>
> Supper was chicken, stuffing, stringbeans, orange cranberry, cottage cheese, & plenty of everything.

202

She will, no doubt, *apologize* for the meal in her next letter—needlessly. But their tiny place was cozy & good. They dont *quite* hit it off—but both have been thru enough to give way to each other—even when impatient. They cd. *never* have mated at an earlier age (he was divorced after 29 yrs of marriage).

Recorded L. reading newer poems . . .

Stayed with them—at their riverside place—till about 7:30 or so. (Given coat/jackets against cold.) Then back here (hotel) for a drink at the bar: . . . Al's play with Shizumi's name . . .

I'd add more detail from memory.

She made it clear that, but for a younger teacher friend across the river, she had no intellectual companionship in the area, and likely never did have any. Her library was wellstocked and ranging. She showed me photos of her father and herself on the river. Told me some of the history of Black Hawk. Al, one-armed (lost his left arm in a machine as a young man), was readily engrossed in the TV. Its main use for her was that it was a distraction for him. They had ample means for their modest existence.

Some children came to the door and Lorine instinctively, very gently, addressed them, went to the icebox and gave them some candybars, left over from Halloween, when they had gone, to her dismay, unclaimed. Al boasted of being frightening to them and was not averse to flashing a gun, if they got too noisy. Lorine naturally shied at his style, but didn't press the issue.

She read poorly, but her eyesight was poor and she was using a magnifying glass to read by and she had never done it before. It was the music on the page that she explored. She read her Jefferson, Morris and Darwin pieces.

At the hotel bar, Al and I had beers and the ladies had Lorine's favorite "grasshoppers" (a *crème de menthe* & ice-cream concoction).

Perhaps a slight sense of her world, or its sense of her, is classically captured in the extended memorial to her in the *Wisconsin State Journal* of Sunday, March 21, 1971, by Joseph McBride, which Al kindly sent me.

It opens:

On New Year's morning the people of this city [Ft. Atkinson] along the Rock River discovered that a poetess had died among them.

A few people knew that Lorine Niedecker [knee-decker, as LZ pronounced it for us] liked to write; they had seen her making notes on the birds while taking her long solitary walks. But even her closest friend, a cousin who had known her since childhood, had never read any of her verse, and still hasn't . . .

Last December, while making lunch in her home on the river, [she] told her husband, "Al, I don't know what's the matter."

Those were her last words. She had suffered a cerebral hemorrhage. Three weeks later, on the morning of Dec. 31, an ambulance took her to a Madison hospital, and by afternoon she was dead . . .

"The people who came to the funeral home said they didn't think her writing would amount to much," her cousin, Mrs. Maude Hartel recalled.

"From what people have told us since she died, I've heard her poetry was rather deep and hard for an ordinary person to understand. Most of the times I was with her, we talked of olden times or of the family."

"After she left, I thought, 'Who is she? And what was she?' " her husband mused as he sat in the living room of the tiny house they built after their marriage in 1962.

They met when Millen—a rough outdoorsman who "rode the freights" out West for years before becoming a building painter in Milwaukee—wanted to buy a cabin she had been given by her father . . .

"The second night I was with her," he said, "she whispered to me she was a poet—a poetess. She thought I might be angry about it.

"Later on, I got the devil bawled out of me when I told somebody in a tavern that my wife was a writer. She didn't want it known. She was bashful."

Some people interpreted her bashfulness as snobbery.

"Hell, I didn't even know the woman," said one of Ft. Atkinson's prominent citizens. "But I heard she had kind of a negative personality."

. . . her father was a carp fisherman and tavern keeper—and cared for her invalid mother after her father's death.

She attended Beloit College and worked briefly as a script writer for WHA radio in Madison. But eventually she returned home and worked in the library and a printing shop, and scrubbed floors in a hospital.

"I was surprised that anyone with the kind of mind she had would have such trivial jobs," said Mrs. Gail Roab. (Roab, who teaches at Ft. Atkinson High School, and his wife were the only "literary friends" she had in town.)

"She told me she didn't mind the jobs, though, because they were just to make a little money for the really important things."

According to Mrs. Roab, the poetess "felt somewhat bad about not being able to communicate" with her neighbors, "but her privacy was self-imposed . . ."

Millen said his wife would "study, study, study" and take endless notes at the kitchen table while he was watching football games on TV. He is a voracious reader of sf (which she didn't like), "but half the junk she read I don't understand.

"I got her to see things and know things," he said. "Every summer we'd go to Canada or North Dakota, Glacier National Park, and so forth. She got over being such a knucklehead about meeting people."

"She was a very young person," Mrs. Roab said. "She was like a bird. I just can't imagine her as being old. Maybe I'm being romantic about her, but that's the way she was. She was a free spirit."

When his wife died, Millen was so "busted up" that he couldn't attend the funeral. She was buried during a blizzard by the minister who had married them. Millen has yet to see her grave.

Her *Collected Poems* 1968 (which finally appeared within a few months of her death) was published by Fulcrum Press in London. No regular publisher in America would take her work on.

Kenneth Cox in England wrote the most extended essay on her a couple of years ago. He says "As first speech-models she remembers 'a happy, outdoor grandfather who somehow somewhere had got hold of nursery and folk rhymes to entrance me' and her mother, 'speaking whole chunks of down-to-earth magic.' "

T&G, the title of a previous collection of hers, was used as her epigraph, out of Lawrence Durrell: "Tenderness and gristle." Her abbreviation makes it seem like a trademark. The Fulcrum Edition unfortunately only goes as far as "Wintergreen Ridge" and her final poems, most of which appear in *Origin* 3rd series #19, have yet to be widely presented. The Darwin poems, from her letters and from her typescript reading for me, came last.

She was embarrassed at being compared to Sappho and Emily Dickinson. Her own words make it amply clear that she prized her work, but was not inclined to exaggerate merit. I can only respect her sense of it.

I think the best critique abides in the poetry itself, as it rises from the page, touches eyes, and sings as it vanishes into other skies. The poems that follow follow in the order she herself set out.

From *My Life by Water:*

PÆAN TO PLACE

Fish
    fowl
        flood
        Water lily mud
My life

in the leaves and on water
My mother and I
        born
in swale and swamp and sworn
to water

My father
thru marsh fog

sculled down
        from high ground
saw her face

at the organ
bore the weight of lake water
        and the cold—
he seined for carp to be sold
that their daughter

might go high
on land
        to learn . . .

.   .   .   .   .   .

He kept us afloat . . .

.   .   .   .   .   .

I grew in green
slide and slant
        of shore and shade
            Child-time—wade
thru weeds

Maples to swing from
Peewee-glissando
        sublime
                slime-
song

Grew riding the river
Books
        at home-pier
            Shelley could steer
as he read

I was the solitary plover
a pencil

for a wing-bone
From the secret notes
I must tilt

upon the pressure
execute and adjust
          In us sea-air rhythm
"We live by the urgent wave
of the verse"

      .   .   .   .   .   .

          . . . what flower
          to take
          to grandfather's grave
unless

water lilies—
he who'd bowed his head
          to grass as he mowed
          Iris now grows
on fill

for the two
and for him
          where they lie
          How much less am I
in the dark than they?

      .   .   .   .   .   .

O my floating life
Do not save love
          for things
               Throw *things*
to the flood

ruined
by the flood
          Leave the new unbought—
          all one in the end—
water . . .

There's a better shine
on the pendulum
than is on my hair
and many times

∙ ∙ ∙

I've seen it there.

∙

Remember my little granite pail?
The handle of it was blue.
Think what's got away in my life—
Was enough to carry me through.

∙

The clothesline post is set
yet no totem-carvings distinguish the Niedecker tribe
from the rest; every seventh day they wash:
worship sun; fear rain, their neighbors' eyes;
raise their hands from ground to sky,
and hang or fall by the whiteness of their all.

∙

Old man who seined
to educate his daughter
sees red Mars rise:
        What lies
behind it?

Cold water business
now starred in Fishes
of dipnet shape
        to ache
thru his arms.

•

You are my friend—
you bring me peaches
and the high bush cranberry
          you carry
my fishpole

you water my worms
you patch my boot
with your mending kit
          nothing in it
but my hand

          •

          FOR PAUL

                    [this would be, of course,
                              Paul Zukofsky]

          Paul
                    when the leaves
                    fall

          from their stems
                    that lie thick
                              on the walk

          in the light
                    of the full note
                              the moon

          playing
                    to leaves
                              when they leave

          the little
                    thin things
                    Paul

                    •

          210

BALLADS

Old Mother turns blue and from us,
    "Don't let my head drop to the earth.
I'm blind and deaf." Death from the heart,
    a thimble in her purse.

"It's a long day since last night.
    Give me space. I need
floors. Wash the floors, Lorine!—
    wash clothes! Weed!"

•

THE YEARS GO BY

Swept snow, Li Po,
by dawn's 40-watt moon
to the road that hies to office
away from home.

Tended my brown little stove
as one would a cow—she gives heat.
Spring—marsh frog-clatter peace
                    breaks out.

•

I rose from marsh mud,
algæ, equisetum, willows,
sweet green, noisy
birds and frogs

to see her wed in the rich
rich silence of the church,
the little white slave-girl
in her diamond fronds.

In aisle and arch
the satin secret collects.
United for life to serve
silver. Possessed.

•

IN EXCHANGE FOR HAIKU

How white the gulls
in grey weather
        Soon April
        the little
yellows

•

New-sawed
clean-smelling house
sweet cedar pink
        flesh tint
I love you

•

Popcorn-can cover
screwed to the wall
over a hole
        so the cold
can't mouse in

•

O late fall
marsh—
        I
raped by the dry
weed stalk

•

HOME/WORLD

My life is hung up
in the flood
    a wave-blurred
            portrait

Don't fall in love
with this face—
    it no longer exists
            in water
                we cannot fish

        •

As I paint the street

I melt the houses
to point up the turreted cupola
I make hoopla

of the low tavern's neon cross—
very like a cross from here—
I honor the huge blue distant dome
valid somehow to the fellow falling high

        •

Alcoholic dream
that ran him
        out from home
            to return

leaning

like the house
in this old part

of town leaves him
        grieving:

why

do I hurt you
whom I love?
    Your ear
        is cold!—here,
drink

            •

NORTH CENTRAL

In every part of every living thing
is stuff that once was rock

In blood the minerals
of the rock

    •

We are what the seas
have made us

longingly immense

the very veery
on the fence

    •

The eye
of the leaf
into leaf
and all parts
        spine
into spine

neverending
        head
to see

•

What cause have you
to run my wreathed
rose words
off

you weed
you pea-blossom weed
in a folk
field

•

For best work
you ought to put forth
            some effort
            to stand
in north woods
among birch

•

Ah your face
but it's whether
you can keep me warm

•

I walked
on New Year's Day

beside the trees
my father now gone planted

evenly following
the road

Each
     spoke

  •

          (Lorine pointed the trees out to us.)
          Full-grown.

from WINTERGREEN RIDGE

. . . Nearby dark wood—

I suddenly heard
    the cry
       my mother's

there the light
    pissed past
       the pistillate cone

how she loved
    closed gentians
       she herself

so closed
    and in this to us peace
       the stabbing

pen
    friend did it
       close to the heart

pierced the woods
    red
       (autumn?)

216

Sometimes it's a pleasure
    to grieve
        or dump

the leaves most brilliant
    as do trees
        when they've no need

of an overload
    of cellulose
        for a cool while

Nobody, nothing
    ever gave me
        greater thing

than time
    unless light
        and silence

which if intense
    makes sound . . .

   .   .   .   .   .

. . . Old sunflower
    you bowed

to no one
    but Great Storm
    of Equinox

   •

The final section (19) of her "Thomas Jefferson" can stand as coda to this little anthology—though I might add my own ending to hers, using words from a letter of hers that I published as a "found" poem in her issue of *Origin*.

Mind leaving, let body leave
Let dome live, spherical dome
and colonnade

Martha (Patsy) stay
"The Committee of Safety
must be warned"

Stay youth—Anne and Ellen
all my books, the bantams
and the seeds of the senega root.

NIEDECKER WEATHER

Well—Milwaukee had
eleven and one
half inches of snow

but no rain. The piles
at street corners are
turning black. Ruskin

would have perished here,
but then, poor man, he
perished anyhow.

Somewhere she says, always into song:

true value expands
it warms.

14 June 1971
Utano

Printed April 1978 in Santa Barbara & Ann Arbor
for the Black Sparrow Press by Mackintosh and Young
& Edwards Brothers Inc. Design by Barbara Martin.
This edition is published in paper wrappers; there
are 500 hardcover trade copies; 200 hardcover copies
are numbered & signed by the author; & 50 numbered
copies have been handbound in boards by Earle Gray,
each containing an original holograph poem by
Cid Corman.

Photo: John Levy

Cid Corman was born in Boston in 1924. He was educated at Boston Latin School and Tufts College. He did postgraduate work at the University of Michigan (where he won a Hopwood Award in 1947), the University of North Carolina, and the Sorbonne. In 1951 he founded *Origin: a quarterly for the creative,* which has recently begun its fourth series. (Corman's anthology, *The Gist of Origin,* has been published by Grossman.) Since 1954 he has lived mostly in Europe and Japan, and still runs Origin Press from his home in Kyoto, where he and his wife also operate an ice cream shop.

Cid Corman has published more than seventy books, many from small presses. Black Sparrow will soon bring out a collection of his poems, *Root Song.*